CANADIAN CHALLENGES

Don Quinlan
Series Editor

Global Links **Connecting Canada**

Robert Kolpin

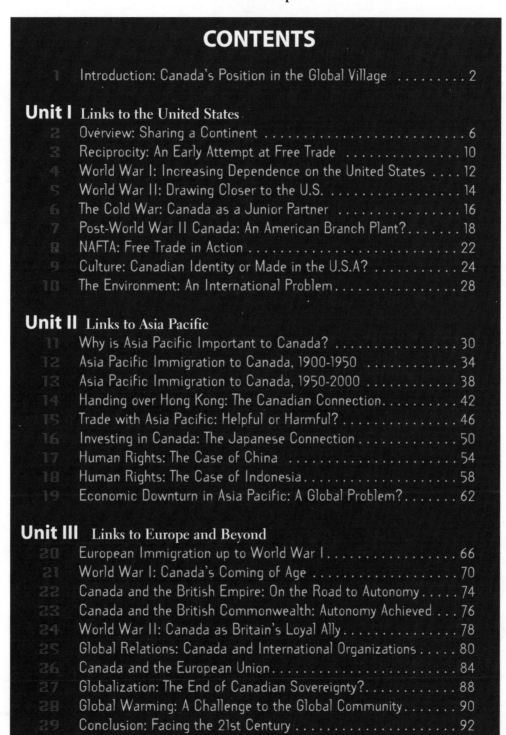

CONTENTS

All terms appearing in boldfaced type in the text are defined in the Glossary that appears on page 96.

FOCUS

This section will help you understand
  a. what is meant by the term "global village"
  b. why Canada has formed strong ties with three regions in the "global village"
  c. the challenges facing Canada in an interdependent world.

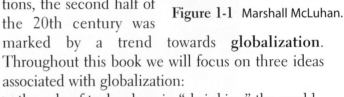

> The new electronic interdependence recreates the world in the image of a global village.
> —Marshall McLuhan in *The Gutenberg Galaxy*, 1962.

Figure 1-1 Marshall McLuhan.

Canada's Global Links

This book focuses on Canada's connections with three areas in the world: the United States, the **Pacific Rim**, and Europe. These three regions have had the greatest impact on Canada's development in the 20th century. By looking at the changing nature of Canada's relationship with these dynamic areas, we can learn a great deal about the international setting in which Canada finds itself today. This is important since the well-being of Canada depends on its **global links**.

In international relations, the second half of the 20th century was marked by a trend towards **globalization**. Throughout this book we will focus on three ideas associated with globalization:

▶ the role of technology in "shrinking" the world,
▶ the advantages and disadvantages of the new **global economy**, and
▶ the way globalization has affected the **quality of life** for people in Canada and around the world.

TIMELINE — 1900-2000

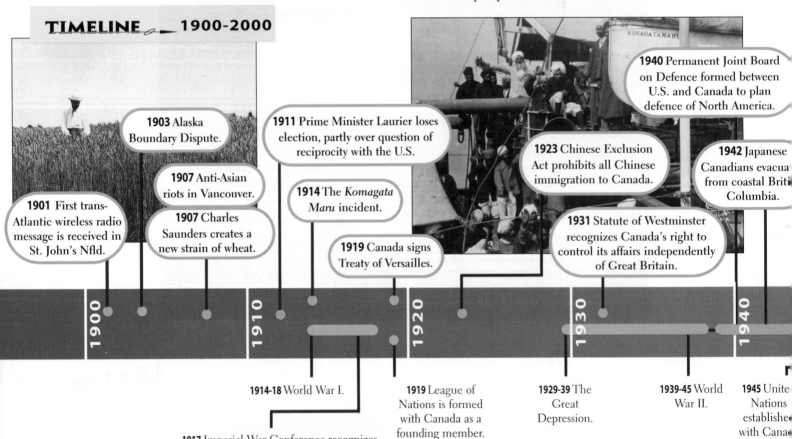

1901 First trans-Atlantic wireless radio message is received in St. John's Nfld.

1903 Alaska Boundary Dispute.

1907 Anti-Asian riots in Vancouver.

1907 Charles Saunders creates a new strain of wheat.

1911 Prime Minister Laurier loses election, partly over question of reciprocity with the U.S.

1914 The *Komagata Maru* incident.

1919 Canada signs Treaty of Versailles.

1923 Chinese Exclusion Act prohibits all Chinese immigration to Canada.

1931 Statute of Westminster recognizes Canada's right to control its affairs independently of Great Britain.

1940 Permanent Joint Board on Defence formed between U.S. and Canada to plan defence of North America.

1942 Japanese Canadians evacua from coastal Briti Columbia.

1900 **1910** **1920** **1930** **1940**

1914-18 World War I.

1917 Imperial War Conference recognizes right of Canada and other Dominions to help make decisions affecting the Commonwealth.

1919 League of Nations is formed with Canada as a founding member.

1929-39 The Great Depression.

1939-45 World War II.

1945 Unite Nations establishe with Cana as a foundi member.

Canada's Position in the Global Village

Canada has the honour of being the second largest country in the world as measured by land area. It is also one of the wealthiest countries with one of the highest **standards of living** in the world. Its wealth means that Canada is eagerly welcomed as a trad-ing partner, and as a market for goods from other countries. It is also a favourite destination for immi-grants from around the world.

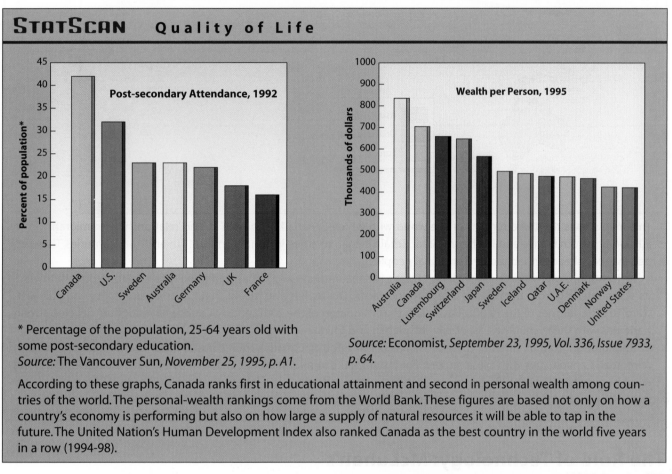

StatScan   Quality of Life

Post-secondary Attendance, 1992

Percent of population*

(Canada, U.S., Sweden, Australia, Germany, UK, France)

* Percentage of the population, 25-64 years old with some post-secondary education.
Source: The Vancouver Sun, *November 25, 1995, p. A1.*

Wealth per Person, 1995

Thousands of dollars

(Australia, Canada, Luxembourg, Switzerland, Japan, Sweden, Iceland, Qatar, U.A.E., Denmark, Norway, United States)

Source: Economist, *September 23, 1995, Vol. 336, Issue 7933, p. 64.*

According to these graphs, Canada ranks first in educational attainment and second in personal wealth among coun-tries of the world. The personal-wealth rankings come from the World Bank. These figures are based not only on how a country's economy is performing but also on how large a supply of natural resources it will be able to tap in the future. The United Nation's Human Development Index also ranked Canada as the best country in the world five years in a row (1994-98).

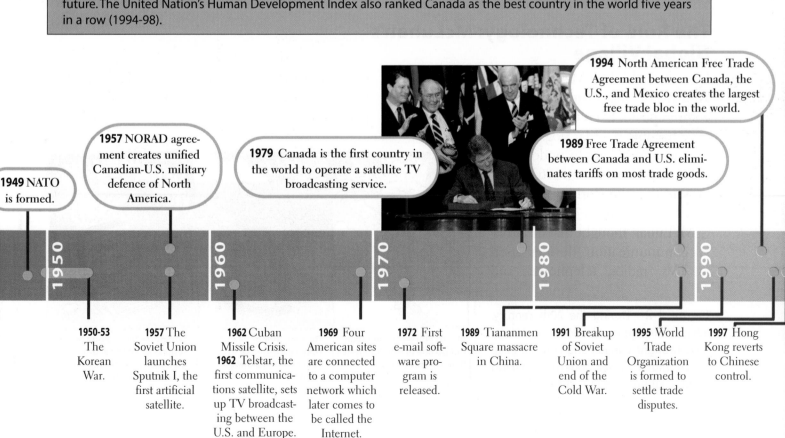

1994 North American Free Trade Agreement between Canada, the U.S., and Mexico creates the largest free trade bloc in the world.

1957 NORAD agree-ment creates unified Canadian-U.S. military defence of North America.

1979 Canada is the first country in the world to operate a satellite TV broadcasting service.

1989 Free Trade Agreement between Canada and U.S. elimi-nates tariffs on most trade goods.

1949 NATO is formed.

1950   1960   1970   1980   1990

1950-53 The Korean War.

1957 The Soviet Union launches Sputnik I, the first artificial satellite.

1962 Cuban Missile Crisis.
1962 Telstar, the first communica-tions satellite, sets up TV broadcast-ing between the U.S. and Europe.

1969 Four American sites are connected to a computer network which later comes to be called the Internet.

1972 First e-mail soft-ware pro-gram is released.

1989 Tiananmen Square massacre in China.

1991 Breakup of Soviet Union and end of the Cold War.

1995 World Trade Organization is formed to settle trade disputes.

1997 Hong Kong reverts to Chinese control.

M a p S t u d y   CANADA'S MOST IMPORTANT GLOBAL LINKS

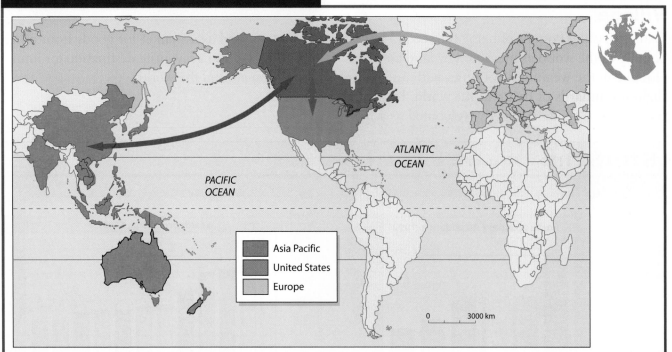

Asia Pacific
United States
Europe

This map shows the three regions of the world with which Canada has formed strong relationships. Immigrants from Europe, first from France and later from Great Britain, began to arrive in Canada in the 17th and 18th centuries. They settled in areas already inhabited by Aboriginal peoples.

Its location, directly north of the United States, has meant that Canada has traditionally felt a strong pull southward. Its size, stretching from the Atlantic Ocean to the Pacific Ocean, has also meant that Canada has felt a strong pull eastward, to the countries of the Pacific Rim area. In the last quarter of the 20th century, Canada has sought to develop strong trade ties with these countries, especially with Japan and China.

Immigration from all three of these areas has contributed to Canada's multicultural make-up. Immigration has also reinforced Canada's ties with these regions. For instance, the immigration to Canada of over 300 000 people from Hong Kong between 1985 and 1996 has given Canada an edge in trading and investment deals with Hong Kong and, therefore, with China as well.

The Role of Technology: McLuhan's Global Village

Canadian thinker Marshall McLuhan was well known for his insights into the ways people communicate. Even though some of his statements have become popular slogans, they are not always easy to understand. What did he mean in 1962 when he said that the world was turning into a "global village?"

McLuhan thought that electronic communication devices such as TVs, radios, telephones, and

computers made the world smaller. They did this by transferring information more quickly from place to place.

Figure 1-2 During the 20th century, advances in communications technology have brought Canada and countries like Japan much closer together, making them neighbours in the global village.

Mount Fuji erupts in Japan but no one in North America hears of this event.	**The radio brings news of Tokyo earthquake to Vancouver in a matter of hours.**	**Computer technology brings reports of Kobe earthquake to Canadian newsrooms in a matter of minutes.**

The Global Economy

Besides information, the other item that can be transferred almost instantly in the global village is money. Investors around the world can now send their money to their country of choice by simply making a telephone call or striking a few keys on the computer. As a result countries have grown more **interdependent**.

In 1998, the Canadian dollar fell sharply against the U.S. dollar. The Bank of Canada tried to stop the dollar's fall by buying millions of Canadian dollars on world currency markets. Despite the Bank's efforts, the dollar continued to slide. Why? Read the following news article that appeared at the time, and then list two reasons to account for the dollar's continued slide.

Quality of Life

The growing interdependence of countries has had a direct impact on the quality of life in many countries. Many people's standard of living has gone up. At the same time, their lives have suffered in other ways.

▶ *human rights*: In the drive to build successful economies, have some governments violated their citizens' human rights?

▶ *the environment*: In the drive for higher profits and lower production costs, have some companies polluted the natural environment?

▶ *culture*: In its drive to find more and more customers for its products, will the United States come to dominate the cultural life of peoples around the world? Will smaller, less wealthy countries lose their unique cultures as a result?

NewsFlash

Dollar dives to record low

By Les Whittington

The loonie's case of Asian flu turned nasty yesterday as the dollar fell to an all-time low against the U.S. buck. The loonie suffered from Bank of Canada governor Gordon Thiessen's acknowledgement Tuesday that the Canadian economy will be battered by the financial upheaval in Asia.

Canada is predicted to have the strongest economy this year of any major industrialized country, but the Canadian dollar has dropped almost 4 per cent against its U.S. counterpart since late September.

This is because investors made jittery by the bank collapses and currency meltdowns in Asian countries have been pouring money into the so-called safe haven of the United States.

In addition, investors who see Canada as dependent on exports of metals, lumber, and other **commodities** have been put off because of the severe decline in commodity sales to Asia. This outlook was unswayed yesterday by a Statistics Canada report that Canada's trade surplus widened to $1.03 billion in November.

Traders said the dollar is likely to come under more pressure in the weeks ahead because of the continuing uncertainties arising from Asia.

Source: *The Toronto Star* (January 22, 1998), p. D1.

Figure 1-3 Students protest in Tiananmen Square on May 25, 1989. On June 4, the Chinese government used troops to crush the student protest. Hundreds of demonstrators were killed and instantly images of the massacre were broadcast around the world. The official policy of the Canadian government has been to overlook human rights violations in China while vigorously pursuing investment opportunities for Canadian companies. Where do you stand on this issue?

RECONNECT

1. In your own words, define the terms interdependent and the global village.

2. What advantages might Canada's multicultural population give it in the global village?

2 Overview: Sharing a Continent

FOCUS

This section will help you understand
  a. that the United States has had a dominating influence on Canada's history, economy, and society in the 20th century
  b. that Canada has had to struggle to maintain its own identity in the face of American influence.

> **Living next to you is in some ways like sleeping with an elephant. No matter how friendly and even-tempered the beast, one is affected by every twitch and grunt.**
> —Prime Minister Pierre Trudeau speaking to American newspaper reporters in Washington D.C., March 25, 1969.

TIMELINE — Canada-U.S. Relations 1900-2000

1903 — Canada loses territory it claimed on the Pacific coast to the U.S. during the Alaska Boundary Dispute.

1911 — Prime Minister Laurier loses election, partly over the question of reciprocity (free trade) with the U.S.

1914-18 — World War I pushes Canada closer to the U.S. as a trading partner.

1922 — For the first time in Canadian history, foreign investment from the U.S. is greater than that from Great Britain.

1939-45 — World War II results in closer Canadian-American cooperation on defence and the economy.

1940 — Canada and the U.S. establish the Permanent Joint Board on Defence to plan defence of North America.

1942 — The Alaska Highway is completed through Canada by the U.S. Army.

1949 — Canada and the U.S. help to form NATO as a defensive alliance against the Soviet bloc.

1957 — NORAD agreement creates a unified Canadian-American military defence of North America.

1962 — NORAD orders the Canadian military on full alert during the Cuban Missile Crisis.

1965 — The Autopact ensures U.S. market for Canadian-built cars.

1974 — The Foreign Investment Review Agency is set up in 1974 under Prime Minister Trudeau to discourage American takeovers in the Canadian economy.

1985 — Canada and the U.S. sign the Pacific Salmon Treaty but are unable to agree on quotas for how many salmon each country can catch in a year.

1989 — The Free Trade Agreement between Canada and the U.S. eliminates cross-border tariffs on most trade goods.

1991 — The U.S. and Canada sign the Air Quality Agreement to cut down on cross-border air pollution and acid rain.

1994 — The North American Free Trade Agreement between Canada, the U.S., and Mexico creates the largest free trade bloc in the world.

1996 — The U.S. passes the Helms-Burton Act which punishes countries like Canada for trading with Cuba.

The Border

The United States has a greater influence on the lives of Canadians than any other country in the world. This is especially true of Canada's history, economy, and society. This is partly because the U.S. and Canada are such close neighbours—the two countries share a border about 6547 kilometres long. The Canadian population is clustered close to the U.S., with 80% of Canadians living within 320 kilometres of the border. Another factor is the size of the U.S., which has the largest economy and the most powerful military machine of any country in the world.

MapStudy CANADIAN POPULATION DENSITY

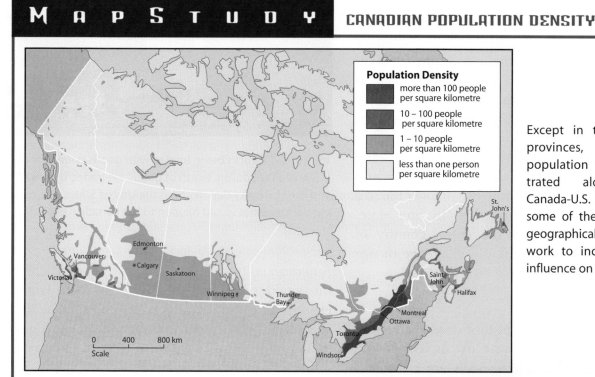

Population Density
- more than 100 people per square kilometre
- 10 – 100 people per square kilometre
- 1 – 10 people per square kilometre
- less than one person per square kilometre

Except in the Prairie provinces, Canada's population is concentrated along the Canada-U.S. border. List some of the ways this geographical fact might work to increase U.S. influence on Canada.

History

American military and political pressure on Canada goes back to the American Revolution when the U.S. declared its independence from Britain while Canada remained loyal to the British Empire. In 1867, fear of the military muscle of the U.S. was one of the main causes of Confederation. Another significant influence consisted of large-scale immigration from the U.S. throughout the 19th and 20th centuries.

Links continued to multiply during the 20th century. Both World War I and II pushed Canada and the U.S. into a growing North American partnership. As Canada gained **autonomy** from Britain, the penetration of American businesses and culture deepened. After World War II, military and political links between Canada and the U.S., such as NATO and NORAD, expanded so much that a small, but increasing number of Canadians began to fear that Canada would lose its independence.

Figure 2-1 *Tory Refugees on Their Way to Canada* by Howard Pyle. American immigration to Canada began with the United Empire Loyalists during the American Revolution. From 1901 to 1911, more than 30% of the immigrants to Canada came from the United States.

The Economy

It would be difficult to find two other countries in the world with more economic links than Canada and the United States. The already enormous trade with the United States has been strengthened further with treaties such as the North American Free Trade Agreement. Signed by Canada, the United States, and Mexico in 1993, it created the largest trading bloc in the world. In 1996 over 77% of Canada's trade was with the United States. The next largest country was Japan which only accounted for about 4.5%. In addition, American companies dominate **sectors** of the Canadian economy such as manufacturing, oil and natural gas, and mining. Sixty-eight percent of all foreign investment in Canada came from the United States in 1996.

But the relationship is hardly one between equals. As the figures below show, the economy and population of the U.S. are roughly 10 times the size of Canada's. More people live in one state, California, than live in the entire country of Canada. How do you think this difference in size affects relations between the two countries?

Society

Canadian society is subject to a steady barrage of American culture. American TV shows, movies, music, books, and magazines entertain Canadians during their leisure hours. Of course, evidence of

Figure 2-2 Trucks being loaded with goods bound for the U.S. Millions of dollars worth of goods are traded by Canada and the U.S. every day. Without the United States as a trading partner, what would happen to the Canadian economy?

American culture can be seen nearly everywhere in the world since the U.S. is the world's largest exporter of cultural products. It is no surprise that Canadians, who share a common language as well as a common border with the U.S., have been so influenced by American culture.

StatScan   Canada and the United States: A Comparison

	Canada	United States
Area (sq. km.)	9 970 610	9 363 520
Total GNP ($U.S. 1995)	543 042 000 000	6 649 806 000 000
Population density (persons per sq. km., 1995)	3	28
Infant mortality rate (per 1000 live births, 1995)	6	9
Military spending ($U.S., 1995)	9 077 000 000	272 066 000 000
Number of active soldiers (1996)	61 336	1 056 000
Passenger cars in use (1995)	13 639 400	137 981 000
Cars produced (1993)	1 100 000	5 700 000
Head of cattle (1996)	13 186 000	103 487 000
Cement (metric tonnes, 1994)	10 584 000	77 900 000

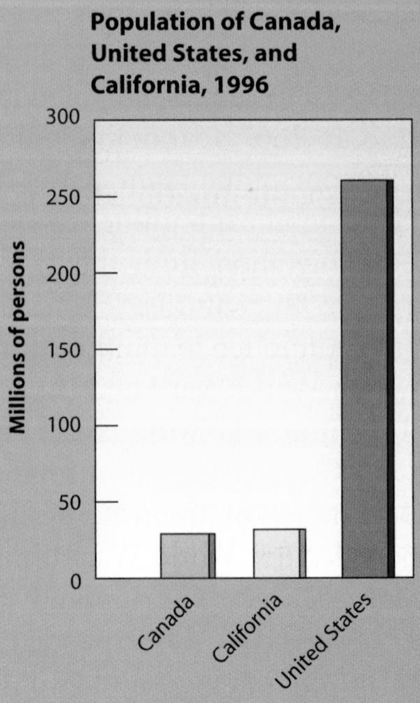

Population of Canada, United States, and California, 1996

(Bar graph: Millions of persons, scale 0 to 300. Canada ~30, California ~32, United States ~265.)

Figure 2-3 Canada's population is less than that of one American state—California.

StatScan
Murder Rates in Canada and the United States, 1996

Compare this chart to the population graph on page 8. In his book, *The Betrayal of Canada,* Canadian nationalist Mel Hurtig wrote, "The 'right to bear arms' in the United States has become a grotesque pollution of the idea of freedom…The number of murders make the statistic from all other nations seem marginal by comparison…"

	Murders
Canada	644
California	2 916
U.S.	19 645

Source: John R. Colombo, The 1998 Canadian Global Almanac, *p. 186. Uniform Crime Reports for the U.S., 1996 (Washington D.C., FBI), pp. 13, 79.*

Figure 2-4 In your opinion, what does this chart indicate about society in the United States in comparison to Canada?

Protecting Canadian Identity

During the 20th century Canada made several attempts to protect itself from the often overpowering influence of the United States. These steps were contrary to the main trend in Canadian-American relations which brought the two North American countries closer together. Some of the more important measures were:

▶ the defeat of Wilfrid Laurier and the Liberal Party in the 1911 election which killed the proposed Reciprocity Treaty (free trade) with the U.S.

▶ the 1968 Watkins Task Force report, Foreign Ownership and the Structure of Canadian Investment, which recommended protecting the Canadian economy from foreign, especially American, **multinational corporations**.

▶ the formation of the Foreign Investment Review Agency in 1974 to discourage American takeovers of the Canadian economy.

▶ the formation of the National Energy Program in 1980 to increase Canadian ownership of Canada's energy supply.

Figure 2-5 Although Canadians as a whole seem fascinated by much of the culture and society of the U.S., there are many aspects they wish to keep at arm's length. These include widespread poverty, the decay of large cities, and ongoing racial conflict.

Foreign Cultural Influences in Canada

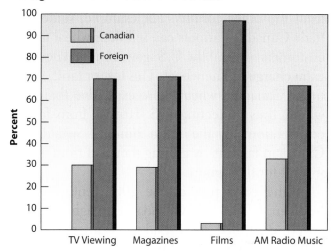

Figure 2-6 This graph contrasts Canadian and foreign content in the entertainment industry in Canada. Most foreign content comes from the U.S. What does this graph say about the future of Canadian culture?

Canadian–American Relations

In this chapter we have seen how political, economic, and cultural issues between Canada and the United States have played a key role in the development of our country. In the following chapters of this unit we will look more closely at Canadian-American relations during the 20 century. To learn how Canada has been influenced by, and reacted to, its superpower neighbour is crucial in understanding Canada's place in the world today.

RECONNECT

1. What evidence is there that the United States plays a dominating role in Canada's affairs?

2. How is Canada's identity challenged by close relations with the U.S.?

FOCUS

This section will help you understand
   a. that reciprocity was an early attempt to establish free trade with the United States
   b. that free trade with the United States was a controversial issue throughout the 20th century.

What is Reciprocity?

Reciprocity is the old word for free trade. When free trade exists between two countries it means that neither country places **tariffs** on goods coming from the other country. For example, under free trade Canadian farmers can sell their wheat to U.S. customers without the U.S. government placing an extra charge on the wheat. This tax, or tariff, would make Canadian wheat more expensive than U.S. wheat, thus protecting U.S. farmers from foreign competition. At the same time, it would hurt Canadian farmers by cutting them off from a large market for their grain.

In the early part of the 20th century, tariffs between the U.S. and Canada were high. The U.S. government, led by President William Howard Taft, offered Canadian Liberal Prime Minister Sir Wilfrid Laurier the International Reciprocal Trade Agreement. If passed by both the U.S. Congress and the Canadian Parliament, it would have given the two governments a reciprocal or mutual agreement not to charge tariffs on each other's products. In Canada this issue created controversy.

Figure 3-1 Prime Minister Sir Wilfrid Laurier.

Opposition to Reciprocity

At first Prime Minister Laurier was sure reciprocity would be a hit with the Canadian people. Once he had the American offer in hand, he called an election for September 1911. Laurier knew reciprocity had strong support among Canadian farmers in the Prairies and lumber companies in British Columbia. Since the proposed agreement eliminated tariffs on **primary goods** such as farm products and lumber, farmers and forestry companies stood to gain new markets for their goods.

In Central Canada and the East, the proposed agreement was not so popular. Even though protective tariffs would remain on most manufactured goods, the business community regarded the agreement with suspicion. Factory owners feared they would have to compete against American manufacturing companies. Since the Americans had a market 10 times the size of that in Canada, they could produce and sell their products for less and still make a profit. Factory workers in Ontario and Quebec feared that unregulated competition would force their factories to close, costing them their jobs.

THE RECIPROCITY TREATY, 1911

This treaty was intended to limit or remove tariffs on products flowing between Canada and the United States. In spite of the claims of Canadians who were against the treaty, it did not mean wholesale free trade. The Reciprocity Treaty would have:

- removed duties on most natural products, including agricultural products such as grain, fruit, vegetables, livestock and fish
- reduced tariffs on products used in farming such as barbed wire and cream separators
- provided the opportunity to negotiate further changes involving other manufactured products.

Soon the opposition Conservative Party waded into the debate. Reciprocity, they said, was a plot by the U.S. government to break Canada's ties with Great Britain and increase U.S. influence over the Canadian government. In fact, they charged that the real goal of the reciprocity agreement was the **annexation** of Canada by the U. S. This last charge loomed much larger in the minds of Canadian voters after several U.S. politicians gave speeches welcoming Canada into the American republic.

Reciprocity and the Election of 1911

By the time the election was held in September 1911, reciprocity had become an emotional issue. Laurier watched as public support for the agreement slipped away, even among a number of prominent Liberal politicians.

On election day, Robert Borden's Conservatives soundly thumped Laurier's Liberals, winning 134 seats to the Liberals' 87. Protective tariffs would remain in place. Canadian manufacturers in Ontario and Quebec had won an important victory. The Western farmers, who showed strong support for Laurier in the election, felt they had been betrayed by the business community in the East. The defeat of reciprocity was one of the seeds of **Western alienation**.

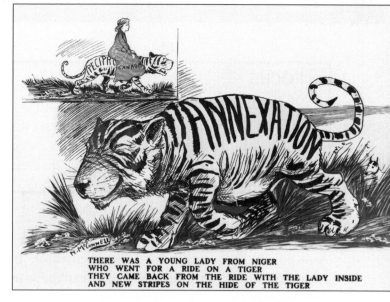

THERE WAS A YOUNG LADY FROM NIGER
WHO WENT FOR A RIDE ON A TIGER
THEY CAME BACK FROM THE RIDE WITH THE LADY INSIDE
AND NEW STRIPES ON THE HIDE OF THE TIGER

Figure 3-2 This cartoon appeared in the *Toronto Daily News* during the 1911 election campaign. Which party did the cartoonist support?

Figure 3-3 Brian Mulroney campaigned on a free trade platform in the 1988 election.

CONNECTIONS

FREE TRADE

The issue of free trade between Canada and the U.S. is older than Canada itself. In 1854, the colonies of British North America signed a Reciprocity Treaty with the U.S. The Americans cancelled this treaty in 1866 because of British support for the South in the U.S. Civil War. The resulting financial hardships for Canadian businesses helped push the colonies of British North America towards Confederation in 1867.

In the election of 1878, opposition leader John A. Macdonald proposed his National Policy with high protective tariffs. Macdonald stumped the country with promises to protect Canadian industry from American competition and preserve Canada's connections with Great Britain.

Thanks to the National Policy, Macdonald's Conservatives won the election easily. In 1911, the defeat of Laurier and the reciprocity agreement meant that the National Policy tariffs would remain in force.

But free trade was an issue that would not go away. In 1988, Conservative Prime Minister Brian Mulroney went to the polls advocating free trade with the U.S. Although most voters cast their ballots against free trade, the vote this time was split among opposition parties and Mulroney was returned to power. This led to Canada's signing of the Free Trade Agreement with the U. S. in 1988 and the North American Free Trade Agreement (NAFTA) with the U.S. and Mexico in 1993.

RECONNECT

1. Summarize the main arguments for and against reciprocity during the election of 1911.

2. Make a timeline that shows the key dates about the issue of free trade between Canada and the U.S. Why has free trade been such an important issue throughout Canada's history?

FOCUS

This section will help you understand
  a. the effect World War I had on the Canadian economy
  b. that during the war Canada shifted from economic dependence on Great Britain to economic dependence on the United States.

Economic Overview

As a country with a vast land mass, a stockpile of untapped natural resources, and a very small population, Canada has had to develop a unique economic structure. Its small population means Canada has an equally small **domestic market** for its goods. Throughout its history, Canada has had to devote a larger share of its economy to trade than most other countries in the world. Much of this trade has been in natural resources, such as lumber, minerals, and fish.

Canada in 1914

When the 20th century opened, Canada had closer economic ties with Great Britain than with any other country in the world. This remained true right up to World War I (1914–1918). In 1901, Canada exported $93 million worth of goods to Great Britain compared to $68 million to the U.S. By 1916, exports to Great Britain were worth $452 million compared to $201 million to the U.S. In 1900, Great Britain accounted for 85% of the foreign investment in Canada. By 1918, foreign investment from Britain was still at 60%.

Besides economic ties, the sentimental connections between Canada and "the mother country" were still very strong in 1914. Most English Canadians thought of Canada less as an independent country than as a self-governing colony within the British Empire.

Despite these connections, Canadians in 1914 were feeling a strong economic pull southwards to the wealthy U.S. Part of this resulted from heavy U.S. immigration to Canada. Between 1901 and 1911, about 32% of all new immigrants to Canada came from the U.S. As early as 1901, Canadian imports from the U.S. had exceeded imports from Great Britain. In the end, the financial pressures caused by World War I forced Canada to look to the U.S. for trade and investment and away from Great Britain.

Figure 4-1 Robert Borden campaigned against reciprocity in the election of 1911. He claimed that Laurier's policy of reciprocity with the U.S. would cut Canada's traditional ties with Great Britain. Borden's campaign slogan was "No truck or trade with the Yankees." During World War I, Borden's Conservative government borrowed large sums of money from American bankers. Soon after the war trade between Canada and the U.S. increased significantly. In your opinion, was Borden justified in breaking his election promise? Back up your opinion with several reasons.

The Cost of War

In August 1914, Canada leaped into a war that most people thought would be over by Christmas. Young Canadians were desperate to "see action" before the war ended, and by the end of August 33 000 had volunteered.

Instead of ending in four months, World War I dragged on for more than four years. The financial and human costs were horrific. As the number of British dead increased, the country's war debt also mushroomed. By the end of the war in 1918, Great Britain had a debt of 275 000 000 pounds and 722 785 had been killed.

World War I and the Problem of Debt

Canada, Britain, France, Germany, Russia, and Austria-Hungary were all involved in World War I from the beginning. In contrast, the U.S. did not declare war on Germany until April 1917. In the meantime, the U.S. reaped great economic benefits as its farms and factories supplied the war machines in Europe. The U.S. also loaned vast amounts of money to the Allied Powers.

When Canada entered the war as a member of the British Empire, Prime Minister Borden assumed that Great Britain would pay for Canada's military contribution. Britain's growing war debt, however, meant it could not do so. The drain of fighting the war and supplying Britain meant that Canada's own debt also increased astronomically. By 1917, Britain could no longer afford to pay for the weapons and food which it had been receiving from Canada since the beginning of the war. As a result, Britain took out huge loans from the U.S. and some of this money ended up in Canada. In addition, Canada had to export large quantities of war materials to the U.S.

Between 1913 and 1918, Canada's national debt swelled from $463 million to $2.46 billion. Canada took a number of steps to control this growing debt. First, it began to finance its war debt through the sale of bonds, which were eagerly bought by Canadian citizens. In 1915, Canadians bought $100 million worth of bonds which was twice the amount expected. In 1917, the government hoped to sell $150 million worth of bonds. The specially issued Victory Bonds brought in $500 million. Second, in 1917 the government for the first time introduced a national income tax. In the end, however, both Canada and Great Britain had to turn for loans to American banks in New York City, which was fast becoming the centre of world finance.

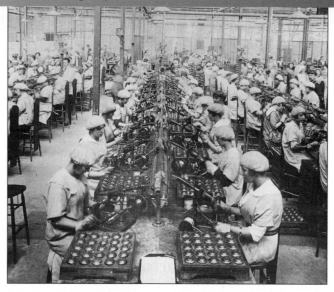

Figure 4-2   This munitions plant produced fuses for the British military during World War I. Britain paid for these fuses by taking out loans with American banks. What effect did this have on links between Canada and Britain and the U.S.?

StatScan   World War I and National Finances

Personal Taxation Rates

	Prewar	Postwar
Britain	9%	27%
U.S.	2%	8%
Canada	11%	13%

Source: from Randal, Gray Chronicle of the First World War, Vol. II: 1917-1921 (New York: Facts on File, 1991).

Figure 4-3   What do the statistics show about the effects of World War I on Britain and the U.S.?

CONNECTIONS

CANADA'S DRIFT TOWARDS THE U.S.

Canada's drift away from Great Britain and towards economic dependence on the U.S. continued throughout the 20th century. In 1922 Canada for the first time in its history received more foreign investment from the U.S. than from Great Britain. In that year the U.S. invested $ 2 593 000 000 while $2 462 000 000 came from Britain. After World War II the U.S. dominated Canada's trade relations. By itself, the U.S. received 80% of Canada's exports and shipped 67% of Canada's imports in 1995.

RECONNECT

1.   How did Canada pay for its war effort during World War I?

2.   How did World War I change the relationship between Canada and Britain and Canada and the U.S.?

FOCUS

This section will help you understand
  a. the effects of World War II on the Canadian economy
  b. why the Canadian economy shifted during the war to an even greater dependence on the U.S.

Between the World Wars

During the Great Depression (1929-1939) the world economy suffered a dramatic downturn. In Canada, unemployment and hardship occurred on a massive scale. The way out of this economic slump only arrived when World War II created a demand for war materials. In Canada the unemployed were finally able to find work, either in war industries or the armed forces.

The Onset of World War II

For Canada there were many parallels between World War I and World War II, especially from an economic view. Strategically, however, the situation Canada found itself in during World War II was more threatening. By June 1940, the French and British military had been swept out of France and across the English Channel to Great Britain.

Figure 5-1 The Blitz was a low point for the Allied cause in World War II. At the time Canada was Britain's main ally.

On July 10 the **Luftwaffe**, the German air force, began strikes on military targets throughout England. This phase of the "Battle of Britain," the contest between the German and British air forces, would last until September 6. Then the Luftwaffe switched to night bombing of civilian targets, especially in and around London. This marked the beginning of the "Blitz," which many people thought would be followed by the German army's invasion of Britain. If Britain fell to the Nazis, how safe would Canada be?

EyeWitness

"1939: Lining up to die"

Anybody saying the war wasn't the end of the Depression just doesn't know what he is talking about, because it was. Somebody once said war is good because every few years it reduces the surplus population. Maybe true, but it sure took a lot of us off the streets and the **rods**. I was in Winnipeg in 1939 in a jungle (temporary camp set up by hobos) where two rivers meet, when war was declared, and when Canada got into it a bunch of us went down to sign up...

I wasn't patriotic. None of my buddies were. I just wanted some good clothes and hot showers and three decent meals a day and a few dollars for tobacco and beer in my pocket, and that's about all I wanted...

So anyway, you know, they decided to line us along the curbs, so we could sit down, and that morning there must have been 500 men if there was a thousand lining about three blocks of curbs away from the armories..., and we just sat in the sun, it was September, and talked.

It was funny, lining up for days to get into a war, to get yourself killed.

—A survivor of the Depression and World War II, quoted in Barry Broadfoot, *Ten Lost Years 1929-1939* (Toronto: Doubleday, 1973), pp. 372-374.

The Permanent Joint Board on Defence

Canada's wartime support for Britain once again forced it to develop closer ties with the United States. When American President Franklin Roosevelt offered to discuss mutual defence issues at Ogdensburg, New York in August 1940, Prime Minister Mackenzie King eagerly accepted. The result of this meeting was the Permanent Joint Board on Defence (PJBD). The PJBD set up a group of military experts to find ways to improve the defence of both countries. In keeping with the "permanent" nature of this body, the PJBD still functions today.

The Lend-Lease Act

The war also encouraged Great Britain and Canada to develop closer ties with the United States in other ways. The best example of this was the Lend-Lease Act, passed by the U.S. Congress in March 1941 before the Americans entered the war in December 1941. President Roosevelt was looking for some way to help Great Britain and her allies, while still keeping the U.S. neutral. The Lend-Lease Act:

▶ gave President Roosevelt the power to send ships, weapons, and war materials to any country thought to be vital to U.S. interests,

▶ set aside an original fund of $7 billion to finance manufacture of these goods,

▶ allowed countries like Britain receiving material through the Lend-Lease program to postpone payment, and

▶ allowed the U.S. to use a number of British-owned military bases.

The Act was of great benefit to Britain, but it created a financial crisis in Canada. It meant that Britain would now turn to the U.S. to buy its war materials, instead of purchasing them from Canada as it had been doing. Canada was on the verge of losing a major source of revenue. It already had a serious **trade deficit** with the U.S. because of all the American products it had bought since the beginning of the war in September 1939.

Figure 5-2 Prime Minister King (far right) and President Roosevelt (centre) attend a church service at Hyde Park, New York in 1944. King and Roosevelt had several meetings during the war. Why do you think Roosevelt was so eager to help Great Britain and Canada even before the U.S. had entered the war?

The Hyde Park Declaration

Prime Minister King moved swiftly to head off the crisis. Only a month after the passage of the Lend-Lease Act, he met with President Roosevelt at Roosevelt's estate in Hyde Park, New York. On April 20, 1941 the two leaders issued the Hyde Park Declaration. This declaration contained two important provisions that saved Canada's war-time economy from ruin:

▶ the U.S. agreed to purchase more military goods from Canada, and

▶ Great Britain was allowed to spend Lend-Lease money on Canadian-produced war materials.

Economic Results of World War II

World War II cemented Canada's economic turn away from Great Britain and towards the U.S. Even though Britain came out of the war victorious, it borrowed so much money during the course of it that the country's economy suffered for years afterwards. The British government was announcing new austerity programs to help balance its trade deficit well into the 1950s. Canada and the U.S., on the other hand, recovered from the war fairly quickly and soon became each other's major trading partner. By 1946, a year after the war, Canadian trade with the U.S. was already three times more than with Britain.

RECONNECT

1. Why did the Lend-Lease Act force Canada into closer economic relations with the U.S.? Explain.

2. Why did Canada draw closer to the U.S. after World War II ended?

The Cold War

After the end of World War II, two superpowers emerged on the world stage: the United States and the Soviet Union. Even though these two countries had fought as allies to defeat Germany and Japan, they soon became bitter enemies after the war. In a sense this was inevitable. These countries had very different systems of government and economics. The United States had a democratic government and a **capitalist** economy. The Soviet Union had a **totalitarian** system of government and a **communist** economic system. The **Cold War** acquired its name because the hostilities between the U.S. and the Soviet Union never erupted into direct open warfare.

The **arms race** was another issue that heightened tensions during the Cold War. The United States had dropped two atomic bombs in 1945 to end the war with Japan. In 1949, the Soviet Union announced it had tested its first atomic bomb. From then on, the two superpowers competed to stockpile ever-larger numbers of nuclear weapons. The Cold War and the arms race did not end until the collapse of the communist systems of government in eastern Europe in the late 1980s and the breakup of the Soviet Union in 1991.

Cold War Links Between Canada and the U.S.

The Cold War strongly influenced Canada's links with the U.S. by increasing the military interdependence between the two countries. This interdependence was especially evident in three alliances or agreements from this period.

NATO   In 1949, Canada and the U.S. were two of the founding members of the North Atlantic Treaty Organization (NATO). The purpose of this alliance was to defend Europe and the North Atlantic region from Soviet aggression. Fourteen countries in western Europe also joined NATO. In response, the Soviet Union and seven eastern European countries signed the Warsaw Pact in 1955, pledging to assist each other in case of attack from the West.

DEW   In 1954, Canada agreed to allow the U.S. to construct a series of 50 radar stations in the Canadian Arctic, roughly along the 70th parallel. The Distant Early Warning (DEW) line would give the U.S. the ability to detect attacking Soviet bombers while they were still far enough away to be intercepted, either by fighter planes or by surface-to-air missiles. The U.S. paid the $250 million needed to build the stations. Although staffed by Canadian military personnel, all recorded information was sent directly to the U.S.

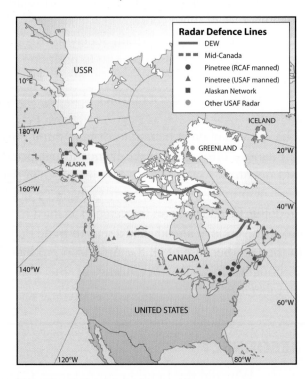

Figure 6-1 The DEW line was the northernmost of three radar defence lines the U.S. established on Canadian territory during the Cold War. Canada was seen by the Americans as the last line of defence in the event of a nuclear attack.

NORAD In 1957, Canada signed a treaty with the U.S. that set up the North American Air Defence (NORAD) system. Under NORAD Canadian and American fighter, missile, and radar units were integrated into a single command to protect North America from Soviet air attacks, especially those involving nuclear weapons. The second-in-command was a Canadian. NORAD headquarters was located in a specially built base under a mountain in Colorado. This underground bunker was designed to protect the NORAD command from a direct nuclear hit.

Tensions Between Canada and the U.S.

Some Canadians were not happy about the closer military ties between Canada and the U.S. NORAD placed 17 000 Canadian Forces personnel and 14 fighter squadrons under the direct command of an American Air Force general. While the consent of both governments was required to put their armed forces on alert, NORAD's headquarters in the U.S. and its American commander highlighted the military superiority of the U.S. Canadian **nationalists** looked on this as a danger to Canadian **sovereignty**.

The problem came to a head in October 1962 during the Cuban Missile Crisis. This was a confrontation between the U.S. and the Soviet Union over the construction of Soviet missile bases in Cuba. When U.S. President John Kennedy set up a naval blockade around Cuba and demanded that the bases be dismantled, the world teetered on the brink of nuclear war.

On October 22, the Canadian Armed Forces were put on Defcon 3 (high military alert or "defensive condition") by Defence Minister Douglas Harkness without prior approval from Prime Minister John Diefenbaker. Harkness thought the situation demanded immediate military alert, but Prime Minister Diefenbaker had stalled at making a decision. He was greatly

Figure 6-2 During the Cold War, Bomarc missiles like this one were placed in Canada under the NORAD agreement with the U.S. But Prime Minister Diefenbaker stalled at arming them with nuclear warheads. After his defeat by Liberal leader Lester Pearson in 1963, 56 of these missiles were armed.

"SOMEBODY UP THERE DOESN'T LIKE US"

Figure 6-3 This cartoon shows President Kennedy with his brother, Attorney-General Robert Kennedy, and Press Secretary Pierre Salinger. What point is the cartoonist making about relations between Kennedy and Diefenbaker?

annoyed at the short notice of the naval blockage given by the American government and resented being pressured by President Kennedy. The Diefenbaker government only officially authorized the Defcon 3 alert two days later. Many Canadians felt Diefenbaker should have done more to support the Americans.

RECONNECT

1. How did the Cold War bring Canada and the U.S. closer together? Name at least two agreements these two countries signed and explain what the agreements did.

2. Was Canada a "junior partner" to the U.S. during the Cold War? Explain your answer.

FOCUS

This section will help you understand
a. how American companies branched into Canada on a large scale after World War II
b. the reaction that took place against American control of parts of the Canadian economy.

The Branch Plant Economy

In the period after World War II the U.S., through financial investments in Canada, came to control or dominate large sectors of the Canadian economy. Let's look at how this happened.

Early in the 1950s, U.S. companies started investing in the Canadian economy. The largest investments came in the **resource sector** of the economy. For instance, American companies made huge investments in Canadian mining projects. The U.S. companies also invested heavily in oil and natural gas exploration, funding pipelines and refineries to process the oil and gas they discovered.

Canada also became a more attractive market for American **retail companies** after the war. This happened for two reasons:
▶ As a result of the post-war **baby boom**, Canada's population grew, making it a larger market for U.S. goods.
▶ Because of an economic boom during the same period, the average Canadian grew wealthier, meaning there was more money to spend on retail goods.
American companies moved quickly to take advantage of these expanding Canadian markets.

Franchises and Branch Plants

The large increase in the American presence in Canada's economy after World War II is connected with the rise of the multinational corporation. American multinationals opened businesses in Canada in two different ways, through **franchises** and **branch plants**.

StatScan
Foreign Investment in Canada, 1945-1997

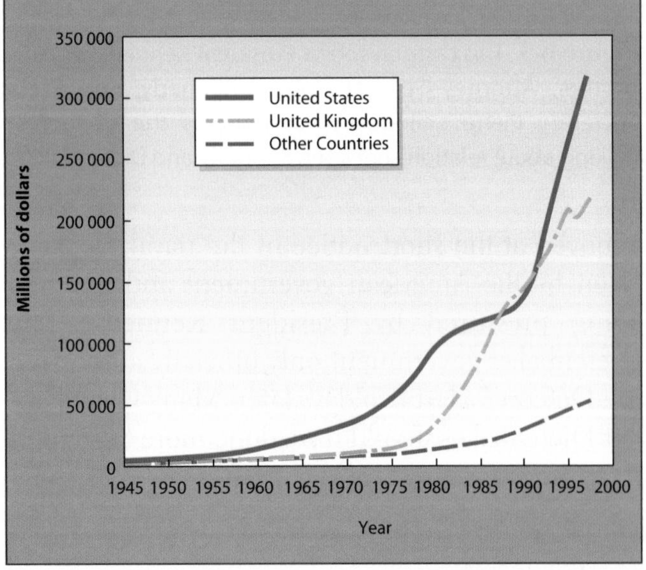

[Graph: y-axis "Millions of dollars" from 0 to 350 000; x-axis "Year" from 1945 to 2000]

Legend:
— United States
-·-·- United Kingdom
– – Other Countries

Figure 7-1 This graph shows how foreign investment, especially from the United States, increased in Canada after World War II. The amounts shown include both direct investment (foreign ownership of companies operating in Canada) and indirect investment (foreign ownership of Canadian securities such as stocks and bonds).

TECHLINK

TV AND THE AMERICANIZATION OF CANADA

In the late 1940s many Canadians living near the American border purchased expensive television sets and erected large antennas in order to receive television signals from the U.S. The first TV stations popular in Canada were all American—NBC, ABC and CBS. It wasn't until 1952 that the Canadian Broadcasting Corporation began its first broadcasts from Toronto and Montreal. By this time, Canadians owned 100 000 television sets; in 1954 the number of TVs topped an incredible one million.

Canadians not only grew to like American TV shows but were also exposed to American advertising. Such mass media advertising paved the way for the rise of **consumerism** in post-World War II Canada.

A franchise is formed when a parent company grants someone a licence to sell its goods. A typical Canadian franchise is a McDonald's restaurant, whose owner pays a licensing fee to sell food under the McDonald's name. The parent company makes an immediate profit from the licensing fee and a long-term profit from the supplies it sells to the owner of the franchise. The Canadian franchise owner makes a profit by capitalizing on the McDonald's name.

A branch plant is a business (often a factory or a retail store) that is owned by a foreign company. A typical branch plant in Canada today is Wal-Mart Canada Inc. This American-owned chain of over 3000 retail stores is one of the largest in the world. In 1994 Wal-Mart bought 122 Canadian stores owned by another American company named Woolco. Since then Wal-Mart has opened another 22 outlets in Canada. Wal-Mart uses its huge buying power and high tech, computer-linked distribution system to sell products at prices which smaller local stores often find impossible to match. By 1998, Wal-Mart had become one of the largest retailers in Canada and employed over 32 500 Canadians.

The Wal-Mart retailing empire is run from its headquarters in Bentonville, Arkansas. From there, it decides where to open new Canadian stores.

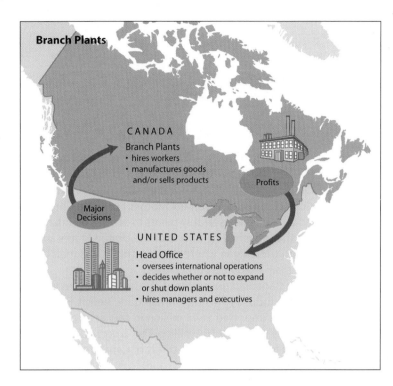

Figure 7-2 For American owners branch plants provide a way of increasing their market share in Canada.

From a Canadian point of view, there are a number of advantages and disadvantages to the branch plant arrangement.

BRANCH PLANTS: FRIEND OR FOE?

Advantages

➟ The branch plant provides jobs for Canadians.

➟ The parent company has to pay Canadian taxes and conform to Canadian labour laws.

➟ The parent company provides investment capital to develop Canadian industry. Sometimes this investment is made at great risk to the parent company.

➟ The parent company often reinvests some of its profits in Canada.

➟ The parent company provides technical know-how that may not be available in Canada. It also supplies the technology itself in the form of parts and machinery.

Disadvantages

➟ Managers can lay off Canadian workers based on the priorities of foreign owners.

➟ Foreign firms with large investments in Canada can pressure governments to grant them exemptions to tax and labour laws or even to change the laws.

➟ Foreign companies may wind up paying lower tax rates than Canadian companies.

➟ Through their investments, foreign companies can gain control over certain sectors of the Canadian economy.

➟ The bulk of the company's profits return to the foreign owners. This outflow of capital weakens the Canadian dollar, making imports more expensive.

➟ Foreign companies often do most of their research in their home countries. In the long-term this can make the Canadian economy dependent on foreign research and technical know-how. It can also lead to a "brain drain" in which highly educated Canadian scientists and engineers seek employment outside Canada.

➟ Foreign companies tend to buy parts from their other plants located in their home countries. This can reduce orders to Canadian companies.

CaseStudy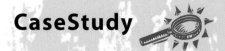

THE AUTOPACT

The automobile industry is the largest manufacturing industry in Canada. Before the arrival of Japanese and Korean car makers in the 1980s, this industry was dominated by the "Big Three" American companies—General Motors, Ford, and Chrysler. They located automobile assembly plants in southern Ontario. This was close to the industrial heartland of the United States and especially to Detroit, Michigan where the "Big Three" had their headquarters and main manufacturing plants.

Figure 7-3 Prime Minister Lester Pearson (left) and President Lyndon Johnson (centre), shown here with Johnson's Secretary of State Dean Rusk, signed the Autopact in 1965.

To the Canadian government, the main problem in Canada's automobile industry was the annual trade deficit. For example, in 1962 Canada imported $642 million in cars and car parts from the U.S. but only exported $62 million. The automobile industry alone accounted for more than two-thirds of Canada's entire trade deficit.

In 1964, Canada opened negotiations with the U.S. with the aim of reducing this yearly trade deficit. It hoped to do this by expanding production of American cars and car parts in Canada and increasing exports to the U.S. This would result in increased employment for Canadian workers in the American branch plants located in Canada. The U.S., on the other hand, hoped to maintain its dominant share of the Canadian market. One way to do this was to eliminate tariffs which American companies had to pay on cars.

On January 16, 1965 Prime Minister Lester Pearson and President Lyndon Johnson signed the Canada-U.S. Automotive Products Agreement, known as the Autopact. Signing the Autopact created a free trade situation in the auto manufacturing sector between Canada and the U.S. It also had two major impacts on auto manufacturing in Canada:

▶ The Autopact enabled car companies like General Motors to coordinate their manufacturing plans between Canada and the U.S. This meant that Canadian auto plants could concentrate on making fewer varieties of cars and parts. This in turn lowered production costs in the Canadian factories.

▶ Lower production costs for Canadian cars and the absence of tariffs on cars coming in from the States translated into lower car prices for Canadian consumers.

The Autopact also had three other important effects:

▶ Over the long-term, it eliminated Canada's automotive trade deficit with the U.S. Between 1965 and 1982, Canada's trade deficit in this industry was more than $12 billion. That changed in the 5-year period between 1982 and 1986 to a surplus for Canada of $22.5 billion. In 1997, Canadians purchased 1.4 million cars but produced 2.4 million for a substantial surplus. Almost 90% of the vehicles manufactured in Canada by American branch plants are exported to either the U.S. or Mexico.

▶ The Autopact led to massive American investment in the Canadian branch plants. Between 1980 and 1986, the American companies spent more than $12 billion on plants and equipment in Canada. In 1997, the Big Three's Canadian motor vehicle plants produced 10 different automobile models and eight different truck and van models.

▶ There have also been substantial job increases in this sector over the years. In 1965, about 70 000 people worked in the Canadian auto industry. By 1986, that number had doubled to 140 000. Ten years later in 1996, almost 150 000 Canadians were employed directly in motor vehicle and automobile parts manufacturing.

On the negative side, critics charge that the industry is still dominated by American companies. As a consequence, they claim that very little money is spent in Canada on research and development.

Figure 7-4 The General Motors assembly plant in Oshawa, Ontario. General Motors Canada is the largest company in the country, but it is also 100% American-owned. In 1997 General Motors employed 29 000 Canadians.

The Debate Over Foreign Ownership

At first the Canadian government did nothing to discourage heavy U.S. investment in Canada. Canadian officials and business leaders felt that Canada needed as much money as possible from outside the country to pay for the country's economic development. Beginning in the 1950s, some Canadians became alarmed over the extent of foreign ownership of Canadian industries. They were especially worried by the way American companies dominated certain sectors of the Canadian economy.

From 1957 to 1972, amid increasing concern over the large amount of foreign ownership in the Canadian economy, the federal government commissioned four reports on foreign investment in Canada. The most important of these, the Watkins Report, was delivered in 1968. Over the next 15 years, it would have far-reaching consequences on the Canadian economy.

StatScan

Foreign Investment: U.S. Control of Canadian Industries

Foreign Ownership, Selected Industries, 1972

Legend:
- % controlled in Canada
- % controlled in U.S.
- % controlled in other countries

Percent (y-axis): 0 to 100

Industries (x-axis): Manufacturing, Oil and Natural Gas, Mining, Railways

Source: Adapted from Historical Statistics of Canada, 2nd ed., Series G291-302 *(Ottawa: Statistics Canada, 1983).*

Figure 7-5 These figures show the extent of foreign ownership in the Canadian economy in 1972. It's unusual for a developed country to have so much foreign control of the economy. What industry was most controlled by companies outside Canada?

CaseStudy

THE WATKINS REPORT AND ECONOMIC NATIONALISM

In 1967, the Canadian government appointed economics Professor Mel Watkins to head a task force investigating the effects of foreign ownership in the Canadian economy. Its report, Foreign Ownership and the Structure of Canadian Investment (1968), documented the large percentage of foreign-owned companies, especially American, in the Canadian economy. This report led to a public debate about the pros and cons of foreign ownership in the economy.

The Watkins Report supported economic nationalists—those who felt that Canadians should control more of their own economy. Underlying the report was the idea that a country with a large share of its economy owned by foreign investors was in danger of losing its independence. To turn back the tide of foreign ownership, Professor Watkins felt the Canadian government had to take action, or intervene, in the economy. During Pierre Trudeau's terms as prime minister, the Canadian government took three steps to strengthen Canadian ownership in the Canadian economy:

- In 1971, the Canadian Development Corporation (CDC) was created to invest in Canadian-owned private companies, especially those involved in petroleum and mining.
- In 1974, the Foreign Investment Review Agency (FIRA) was set up to screen foreign takeovers of Canadian businesses as well as the entry of new foreign businesses into Canada.
- In 1980, the National Energy Program (NEP) was established. It expanded government-owned Petro-Canada so that the government controlled a greater share of Canada's oil resources.

Figure 7-6 Mel Watkins.

Economic nationalists suffered a setback when these programs were dismantled soon after Conservative Brian Mulroney became prime minister in 1984.

RECONNECT

1. Why did American companies start to invest so heavily in Canada after World War II? Give three reasons.

2. Summarize the main arguments for and against foreign ownership in the Canadian economy. Outline your personal views on this issue.

FOCUS

This section will help you understand
a.   the key features of the NAFTA treaty between Canada, the United States, and Mexico
b.   why NAFTA was such a controversial issue in Canada.

The Move to Free Trade

The 1980s witnessed a shift in the way the Canadian government dealt with the economy. This occurred in response to the severe **recession**, or sharp downturn in the economy, during the early 1980s. Political parties debated what the Canadian government should do to help the increasing numbers of unemployed workers and businesses teetering on bankruptcy because of the recession. In the 1984 election, Conservative Brian Mulroney ran on a platform which included abolishing many of the agencies established by previous Liberal governments, such as the Foreign Investment Review Agency (FIRA) and the National Energy Program (NEP). Mulroney asserted that this kind of intervention in the economy discouraged foreign investors from investing in Canada. He felt that with more foreign investment, the economy would revive. Soon after winning the election Prime Minister Mulroney scrapped FIRA and replaced it with Investment Canada, and dismantled the NEP.

The next step Mulroney took was to sign a Free Trade Agreement (FTA) with the U.S. in 1988. The purpose of this treaty was to eliminate tariffs on trade between Canada and the U.S. The FTA became the most important issue in the election of 1988. Though Mulroney's voter support declined significantly, his Conservative Party still managed to win a majority in the House of Commons. As a result, the FTA, which gave both Canada and the U.S. easier access to each other's markets, came into effect on January 1, 1989.

On January 1, 1994 the FTA was expanded to include Mexico. The resulting North American Free Trade Agreement (NAFTA) united all of North America into the largest free trade zone in the world with a total population of approximately 394 million (1997 est.). NAFTA guarantees that Canada and the U.S. will remain each other's most important trading partner, but it does not change the fact that this is still an unequal relationship, with the U.S. economy roughly 10 times larger than Canada's.

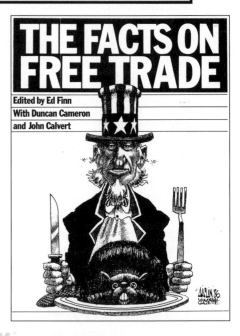

Figure 8-1 The Free Trade Agreement in the 1980s stirred up just as much debate as the Reciprocity Treaty had in 1911. This cartoon appeared in 1988 when the national debate over free trade was reaching a fevered pitch. What symbols are used in this cartoon? What is the cartoonist's opinion of free trade?

CaseStudy
WHAT IS FREE TRADE?

Free trade can be defined as the absence of tariffs on imported goods. A tariff is a **duty** or tax on imports. Its purpose is to make foreign goods more expensive to buy than domestic or locally produced goods. A tariff designed to protect local companies from cheaper imports is called a protective tariff. Since free trade removes these tariffs, it has the effect of making many foreign products cheaper and, therefore, more desirable to buy. The aim of free trade is to increase the number of imports and exports between countries.

Here is an illustration of the way free trade makes imported goods cheaper.

Without Free Trade

Price of foreign		Price of Canadian	
product	$10.00	product	$11.75
Tariff 25%	2.50	No tariff	0.00
Cost to buyer	$12.50	Cost to buyer	$11.75

With Free Trade

Price of foreign		Price of Canadian	
product	$10.00	product	$11.75
No tariff	0.00	No tariff	0.00
Cost to buyer	$10.00	Cost to buyer	$11.75

The Free Trade Debate

In Canada the strongest push for free trade has come from the business community. People who argue for free trade between Canada and the U.S. are often called **continentalists** because they look at the economy from the viewpoint of the entire North American continent. NAFTA grants Canadian exporters access to the huge American market without the threat of high American tariffs. Another benefit is that tariff-free American products are cheaper for Canadians to buy. Finally, continentalists argue that globalization has led many other regions of the world to join in free trade zones. If Canada did not join one, they say, it would be unable to compete internationally.

Critics of NAFTA argue that Canada's economy is already dominated by the U.S. They fear that NAFTA will expand American domination even more. This is called the nationalist position. Nationalists fear that NAFTA will force many Canadian companies into bankruptcy. At the very least, NAFTA will pressure companies to lay off workers or reduce their wages.

KEY FEATURES OF NAFTA

- Eliminates all tariffs by 2008 (with most eliminated well before this date).
- Prevents member countries from setting a quota or limit on imports.
- Makes it easier for each of the three countries to start or buy companies in the other two countries.
- Keeps in place the Autopact's duty-free trade in cars and car parts; Mexico has to remove all quotas and duties on cars and car parts.
- Allows foreign investment in banks and oil and energy plants.
- Protects music recordings and movies from use without permission for a minimum 50-year period.

They claim that tax-supported social programs like the Canadian Medical Plan and Employment Insurance would come under attack by businesses pressuring government to reduce taxes. Finally, Canada's very independence would be endangered by the increasing pull towards the U.S. created by treaties like NAFTA.

CROSSFIRE

DOES FREE TRADE BENEFIT OR HARM CANADA?

Free Trade Benefits Canada

By the time this agreement (the FTA) takes full effect a decade from now, the average Canadian is going to find that he has more money in his pocket, and a wider choice of competitively priced goods and services on which to spend that money. And he will find, too, that he has a better job, a more interesting job, a more secure job—and he will be getting paid more to do it.

—Simon Reisman, chief Canadian trade negotiator for the Free Trade Agreement, quoted in *Free Trade, Free Canada,* ed. Earle Gray (Woodville: Canadian Speeches, 1988), pp. 39-41.

Figure 8-2
Simon Reisman.

Free Trade Harms Canada

We would like to think we are about to get the best of both worlds—Canadian stability and a more caring society, along with American markets, but what if instead we get their crime rate, health programs, and gun laws, and they get our markets—or what is left of them?

—Margaret Atwood, Canadian writer, quoted in *The Facts on Free Trade,* ed. Ed Finn (Toronto: Lorimer, 1988), p. 14.

Figure 8-3
Margaret Atwood.

RECONNECT

1. How has NAFTA changed the Canadian economy? Name specific ways.
2. Summarize the main arguments for and against free trade between Canada and the U.S.

Culture: Canadian Identity or Made in the U.S.A.?

Canadian Identity Versus American Culture

Living next to the United States means that Canadians are neighbours of the largest exporter of culture in the world. People in every corner of the globe wear denim jeans, drink Coca-Cola, watch American TV shows and movies, and listen to American pop music. But no country in the world except Canada shares a border with the U.S. that is 6457 kilometres long. Mere size gives the U.S. an advantage over Canada in the cultural realm. American influences have become so much a part of Canadian life, that many Canadians barely recognize them as coming from another country.

Central to this issue is the question: What does it mean to be a Canadian? It is obvious that Canadians have a different history from their American neighbours and that they live in a different geographical environment. Polls have shown that Canadians consistently view current issues in different ways than people do in the U.S. For example, a poll of 6000 Canadians conducted in October 1996 by the polling company, Angus Reid, showed that 56% of Canadians would be more likely to vote for a political leader who was a Muslim, atheist, or evangelical Christian compared to 33% of Americans. History, geography, and public opinion work together to form a distinct Canadian culture. The question is how to protect this culture from being overwhelmed by the U.S.

Figure 9-1 What do these photos reveal about the American influence on Canadian culture? Taken together, do they indicate a possible danger to Canada? Why or why not?

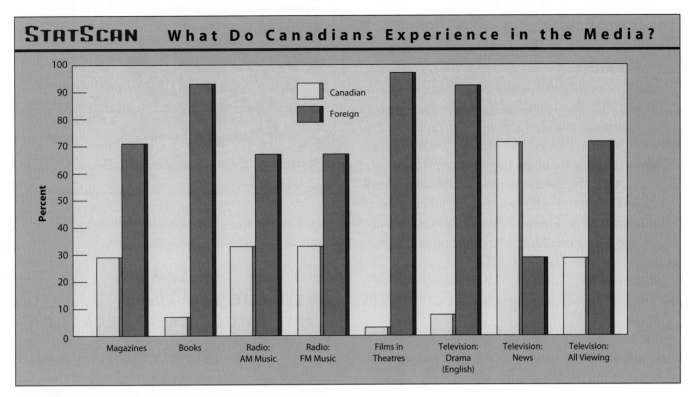

Figure 9-2 What does this graph show about the reading, listening, and viewing habits of Canadians? What does it mean for Canadian culture?

Primary Source
DOES FREE TRADE THREATEN CANADIAN CULTURE?

What does the deal say about culture?

To start with, it says our cultural industries are exempt from the terms of the agreement. This sounds not too bad. Under the deal, Americans can buy up just about any business in Canada, and we, through our government, can't stop them or place conditions on their purchase. If they try to buy a book publisher or other cultural "enterprise" though, our government retains the right to step in.

But the *very next sentence* says, if any Canadian cultural policy cost the Americans money in Canada, the U.S. can retaliate against our exports, and not just in culture, but *in any area they choose*. Talk about giving with one hand and taking back with the other! This is like being told: you can rob that corner store, but if you do you'll go to jail.

This retaliation clause means that if a Canadian publishing house is bought by an American conglomerate…our government can step in and stop the sale. But the Americans have every right then to tote up their financial loss, and hit us back by penalizing Canadian exports to the U.S., such as steel, fish, or agriculture. This is what our government has agreed to, with *no* apparent right of objection or appeal

—Rick Salutin, "What Kind of Canada," from *The Facts on Free Trade*, ed. Ed Finn (Toronto: Lorimer, 1988.), pp. 82-85.

Attempts to Curb American Influence

Taking action against American influences on Canadian culture is not new. Throughout the 20th century, the Canadian government sponsored a number of attempts to curb this American influence. These measures resulted from the fear that without a strong Canadian identity, the survival of Canada as an independent country could be in doubt.

The CBC

Because American radio programs dominated Canadian airwaves during the 1920s and 1930s, the federal government created the Canadian Broadcasting Corporation (CBC) in 1936. This gave Canadians, for the first time, access to Canadian programs on the radio. The new station started with only six hours of broadcasting a day, but a year later this was increased to 16. After the end of World War II (1945), the new **medium** of television created another threat to Canadian culture. By 1950, Canadians owned several thousand television sets, and 100% of the programs they watched came from the U.S.

Figure 9-3 What does this editorial cartoonist think about the drive to save Canadian culture from American influences? Do you agree or disagree with the cartoonist's viewpoint? Support your opinion with reasons.

The Royal Commission on National Development in the Arts and Letters and Sciences

Concern over the amount of American content on Canadian television led to the government setting up a Royal Commission in 1949. Future Governor General Vincent Massey headed the Royal Commission on National Development in the Arts and Letters and Sciences, which warned in its report that Canadian culture was threatened with an "American invasion by film, radio, and periodicals." As a direct result of this report, the government took the following actions:

▶ granted more financial aid to researchers and universities,

▶ directed the CBC to open the first Canadian TV station in 1952, and

▶ established the Canada Council in 1957 to award grants to artists, writers, and other people contributing to Canadian culture.

The Canada Council for the Arts, Humanities, and Social Sciences

The Canada Council was established in order to "foster and promote the study and enjoyment of, and the production of works in, the arts, humanities, and social sciences…" (Canada Council Act, March 28, 1957). In 1978, the Canada Council was changed to focus entirely on the arts. Over the years the Canada Council has provided financial grants to support Canadian novelists, poets, musicians, dancers, singers, and visual artists. It has also funded touring performances by theatre and dancing groups, and symphony orchestras as well as art exhibitions. Many artists who have received financial support early in their careers have become internationally famous. Canada Council grants have supported:

▶ writers like Margaret Atwood, Timothy Findley, Anne Hebert, Joy Kogawa, Michael Ondaatje, Michael Tremblay, W.O. Mitchell, Leonard Cohen, Evelyn Lau, and Rohinton Mistry,

▶ artistic organizations like the National Ballet Guild of Canada, the Stratford Shakespearean Festival, Vancouver Festival Society, The Royal Winnipeg Ballet, Jeunesses Musicales du Canada, and the Toronto Symphony Orchestra

▶ an art bank which collected contemporary Canadian art,

▶ a fund which compensates authors whose books are loaned to the public by libraries,

▶ approximately 3000 professional art organizations and 1200 individual artists annually during the 1990s, and

CaseStudy
HOLLYWOOD CREATES CANADA

During Hollywood's first 50 years Americans made a surprisingly large number of films about Canada. Since 1910 Hollywood has produced more than 500 movies about Canada. By the 1950s, Americans produced about 10 times more feature films about Canada than Canadians had. Most of these films were shot either in Hollywood studios or the California countryside. They portrayed Canada as a snowy wilderness populated by fur traders, Aboriginal peoples, lumberjacks, and Mounties.

Pierre Berton, in his 1975 bestseller *Hollywood's Canada*, had this to say about the "brainwashing" of Canadians by Hollywood film producers:

"No nation as young as ours can be exposed to as many movies over as many years without being brainwashed to some extent by a message that has never really changed. And that's the remarkable aspect of these movies—the consistency of the message. You Canadians, the message keeps telling us, are really just northern versions of Americans: you have no distinctive personality apart from ours, and no distinctive culture, apart from ours. Your identity is our identity. You're quainter, of course, and less sophisticated; but apart from those quirks you're just like us."

—*Pierre Berton*, Hollywood's Canada: The Americanization of Our National Image *(Toronto: McClelland and Stewart, 1975), p.231.*

Figure 9-4 A scene from *Way Down East.* Do you agree with Berton's assessment that Canadians have been brainwashed by American films into thinking that they are just like Americans?

▶ awards for artistic excellence such as the Governor General Literary Award.

The Canada Council is the primary method by which the federal government supports Canadian culture. Like the CBC during the 1990s, its budget has also been reduced as a cost-cutting measure by the government.

CaseStudy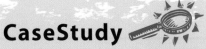

MADE IN CANADA

During the 1990s American movie and TV producers flocked to Canada, especially to British Columbia and Ontario, and spent millions of dollars. Vancouver has even earned a reputation as Hollywood North. One of the main attractions is the low Canadian dollar which allows American filmmakers to produce movies and TV shows more cheaply than in the United States. Popular shows like *The X-Files*, which was shot in Vancouver from 1993 to 1997, employ highly-skilled Canadian workers; everyone from camera crews to actors.

Nearly all of these films or TV shows portray events taking place in the U.S. Street signs, licence plates, and police cars for example, are all changed to reflect American locations. What are the benefits of made-in-Canada American movies and TV shows? Does this have an influence on Canadian culture? Explain your answer.

Figure 9-5 FBI agents Fox Mulder and Dana Scully investigate alien forces during a scene from *The X-Files*.

TECHLINK

DOES THE INTERNET THREATEN CANADIAN CULTURE?

The Internet presents a new and difficult challenge to those who want to protect Canadian culture. Through the Internet information can be delivered virtually anywhere in the world simultaneously. In important ways this "information highway" makes national borders nearly meaningless to anyone with a computer and a modem. Use of the Internet, especially the World Wide Web, is growing by almost 100 percent every year. By January 2000 it is forecast that 377 million users will be communicating through the Internet. Internet usage stands at:

- Canada   4.53 million (Nov. 1997)
- U.S.   55 million (June 1998)
- World   102 million (Jan. 1998)

To Internet users around the world, American Web sites provide American content for surfing and downloading. Some cultural nationalists argue that the Internet will provide another way to dilute Canadian culture in an American electronic ocean. Others point out that the Internet is not one-way communication like TV or the movies. Perhaps, they say, the two-way nature of communication on the Internet might present the

opportunity to project Canadian culture rather than simply absorb American culture. Or, as some experts claim, perhaps a global culture will result from the information highway. The verdict is still to be determined.

In a poll conducted by the polling company, Pollara, in February 1997, Canadians were asked if it will be possible to continue to protect Canadian culture or will new electronic technologies make it impossible to protect Canadian cultural industries.

The national results were:

- impossible   48%
- possible   39%
- don't know   13%

Figure 9-6 Through the Internet, information can travel from one corner of the globe to another in a matter of minutes.

RECONNECT

1. Has the United States exerted an overwhelming influence on Canadian culture throughout the 20th century? Support your answer by referring to evidence in this section.

2. What measures have been taken in Canada to protect our culture from American influence? Do you think these measures have succeeded? Why or why not?

3. How has the Internet changed the cultural landscape in Canada?

FOCUS

This section will help you understand
a. that Canada and the U.S. share many environmental problems in common
b. that cooperation between these countries is necessary to solve their environmental problems.

Environmental Crises in North America

Canada and the U.S. face a number of environmentally hazardous situations. In the past, the two countries have cooperated with each other to solve some of these problems. To combat the problem of acid rain for example, Canada and the U.S. signed the Air Quality Agreement in 1991. This agreement has lowered emissions of sulphur dioxide (one of the main ingredients in acid rain) from industrial smokestacks on both sides of the border. The result has been that some lakes and forests in eastern Canada and New England have now started to recover from acid rain damage.

Save the Salmon: A North American Dispute

Not all the environmental problems the two countries share have been so easily solved. A Canadian-American dispute over salmon has led both to financial hardship for West Coast fishers and to the collapse of some Pacific salmon stocks.

In 1985, Canada and the U.S. signed the Pacific Salmon Treaty. The goal of this treaty was to conserve and enhance each country's salmon stocks. It stipulated that each country's annual catch of salmon should be in proportion to the number of fish that had spawned in the country's waters. The problem is that both Canadian and American-spawned salmon spend much of their life cycle in each other's waters in the Pacific Ocean. According to the treaty, the number of American-spawned salmon caught by B.C. fishers should equal the number of Canadian-spawned salmon caught by American fishers. But from 1985 to 1996, American fishers had intercepted approximately 35 million more salmon originating in Canadian waters (a catch worth about $500 million) than Canadian fishers had caught from American stocks.

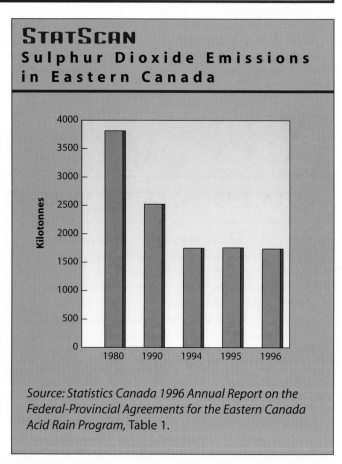

StatScan

Sulphur Dioxide Emissions in Eastern Canada

Source: Statistics Canada 1996 Annual Report on the Federal-Provincial Agreements for the Eastern Canada Acid Rain Program, Table 1.

Figure 10-1 This graph charts the total sulphur dioxide emissions in Eastern Canada between 1980 and 1996 in kilotonnes. The target level set by the provincial and federal governments was 2340 kilotonnes per year. When did Canada reach this figure? Why is reduction of Canadian emissions alone not enough to solve the acid rain problem?

The trouble with the Pacific Salmon Treaty was that neither country could agree on the numbers for the allowable annual catch. They said the details would be worked out later. The result has been that no quotas have been set for a number of years. This dispute erupted once again in 1997 when the Canadian government severely reduced the allowable catch for B.C. fishers to conserve coho salmon stocks. Canadian scientists had determined the coho were in danger of extinction from some northern B.C. rivers. Washington and Oregon agreed to quotas, but the state of Alaska claimed Canadian scientists were wrong and refused to limit their catch of coho salmon. This dispute threatens the livelihoods of approximately 6000 salmon fishers in the province as well as thousands more who are employed in the sports fishery industry.

MapStudy   MIGRATION ROUTE OF PACIFIC SALMON

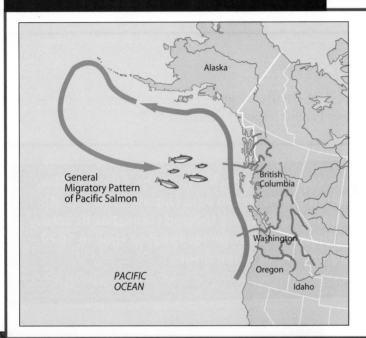

This map shows the migration route of salmon from British Columbia, Alaska, Washington, and Oregon. Many of these salmon spawn in the tributaries of the Fraser River and other B.C. rivers. As part of their life cycle, they migrate to the Pacific Ocean, where they spend considerable time in American waters. Why is an international agreement necessary to ensure the survival of B.C. salmon?

Figure 10-2 During the 1997 "fishing war," salmon fishers from B.C. protested by blockading an American ferry from Alaska in Prince Rupert harbour on July 20, 1997. The B.C. fishers blamed Alaska fishers for taking too many B.C. salmon and the Canadian government for not putting more pressure on the U.S. to negotiate a fair settlement of the Salmon Treaty. Do you think B.C. fishers were justified in making this sort of illegal protest? Why or why not?

Figure 10-3 This cartoon refers to B.C. Premier Glen Clark and U.S. President Bill Clinton. What is the cartoonist suggesting? Do you agree? Why or why not?

RECONNECT

1. Briefly describe two environmental issues facing Canada and the U.S. In your view, which is most important? Why?

Why is Asia Pacific Important to Canada?

FOCUS

This section will help you understand
a. which countries are included in the Asia Pacific region
b. the economic importance of the Asia Pacific region to Canada.

> In 1983, for the first time, more Canadian trade crossed the Pacific than the Atlantic. Now, five of our top 10 trade partners, after the United States, are in Asia (Japan, China, South Korea, Hong Kong and Taiwan)... Even before transpacific trade topped transatlantic trade, more immigrants arrived in Canada from Asia than from Europe for the first time in 1979. Today, over 2 million Canadians are of Asian origin.
> —Lloyd Axworthy, Canadian Minister of Foreign Affairs, March 24, 1997.

TIMELINE 1900-2000

1900 — By 1900, there were 4738 Japanese immigrants and 17 312 Chinese immigrants living in British Columbia.

1904 — The head tax on Chinese immigrants is increased from $100 to $500.

1905-08 — About 2000 Indian immigrants, mostly Sikhs, arrive to work in B.C. sawmills.

1907 — Vancouver is rocked by anti-Asian riot.

1908 — At Canada's request, Japan makes a "gentlemen's agreement" to limit the number of Japanese immigrants to 400 a year.

1914 — The steamer *Komagata Maru*, with 376 Sikh immigrants, is turned away from Vancouver harbour after waiting for two months to disembark its passengers.

1914-18 — World War I.

1923 — Canada passes the Chinese Exclusion Act, which bans all Chinese except students, merchants, and diplomats from entering Canada.

1939-45 — World War II. By its end, Japan is in ruins, both physically and economically.

1942 — Japanese Canadians are evacuated from the West Coast and interned in labour camps in interior British Columbia and Alberta.

1947 — Chinese and Indian Canadians are granted the right to vote in federal elections.

1949 — Japanese Canadians are allowed to return to the West Coast and are granted the right to vote in federal elections .

1986 — Honda starts production of cars in Alliston, Ontario.

1988 — Toyota starts production of cars in Cambridge, Ontario.
The Canadian government apologizes to Japanese Canadians for their treatment during WW II.

1989 — Suzuki, in a joint venture with General Motors, starts production of sports utility vehicles in Ingersoll, Ontario. Pro-democracy demonstrators are massacred in Tiananmen Square in Beijing, China.

1997 — The British return Hong Kong to Chinese rule.

1998 — Census figures reveal Chinese is the third language most often spoken in Canada.
The Asian economic collapse puts pressure on the Canadian dollar and economy.

The West Coast

Canada's West Coast has been presented with a major opportunity to take advantage of the economic growth experienced by the Asia Pacific region in the 1980s and 1990s. The expanding economies of the countries in this region formed one of the most important global trends of the second half of the 20th century. During this period, the economies of several Asia Pacific countries managed to outperform those of North America and Europe. For example, China, South Korea, Malaysia, Singapore, and Thailand all averaged over 8% growth (of GDP) every year between 1986 and 1996. For the same period, Canada and the U.S. experienced growth of only 1.6% and 2.2%.

Between 1960 and 1990, Japan led the charge in the Asia Pacific region. While Japan has the largest economy in the Asia Pacific, other countries in the region surpassed Japan's growth rate in the 1980s and 1990s. For example, South Korea had an average yearly economic growth of 8.1% (of GDP) between 1986 and 1996 while Japan only experienced 2.9%. In fact, Singapore, South Korea, Taiwan, and Hong Kong industrialized so quickly they became known as "the Four Tigers." During the early 1990s, thanks to its liberalized economic policies and a population of more than 1 billion,

Figure 11-1 Autos are unloaded from a Japanese ship in New Westminster, B.C. while paper products are loaded onto a ship in Vancouver bound for export. What benefits does this trade bring to Canada? Are there any drawbacks you could identify?

China's economy developed at a feverish pace. This trend was strengthened by massive foreign investment in the late 1990s and by Britain's return of Hong Kong to China in 1997.

Other countries in the region, such as Malaysia, Indonesia, and Thailand, have also enjoyed significant economic growth, to a large extent because of the development and exploitation of their natural resources.

M A P S T U D Y   THE COUNTRIES OF ASIA PACIFIC

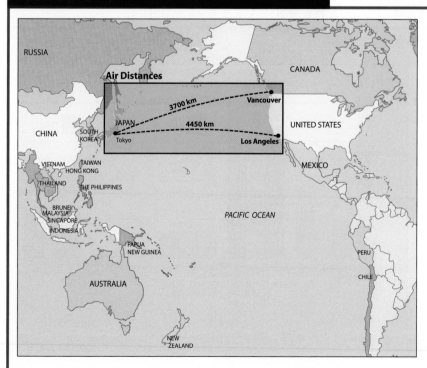

Air Distances

3700 km — Vancouver
JAPAN — 4450 km
Tokyo — Los Angeles

RUSSIA
CANADA
CHINA
SOUTH KOREA
UNITED STATES
VIETNAM
TAIWAN
HONG KONG
MEXICO
THAILAND
THE PHILIPPINES
BRUNEI
MALAYSIA
SINGAPORE
PACIFIC OCEAN
INDONESIA
PAPUA NEW GUINEA
PERU
CHILE
AUSTRALIA
NEW ZEALAND

Asia Pacific is a region that consists of the Asian countries on the Pacific Rim, the circle of land that surrounds the Pacific Ocean. Sometimes countries in Southeast Asia as well as other countries, such as India, are also included in the Asia Pacific region.

This map shows the member countries of the Asia-Pacific Economic Co-operation (APEC), the most important international organization dealing with trade and investment issues in this region. The countries belonging to APEC are in Asia and the Pacific which include such countries as Chile, Peru, and Australia. Canada's trade links with this part of the world have been growing at a faster rate than with any other region. Using this map, make a list of the countries in the Asia Pacific region.

Opportunities in Asia Pacific: Trade and Immigration

Canada has a number of natural advantages that resulted in greatly expanded trade with Asia Pacific countries.

▶ First, Canada has large stocks of natural resources, such as lumber and coal. These materials are in great demand by the expanding industries of Asia Pacific countries. For instance, in 1993 Japan imported more than 50% of the lumber it used that year from Canada.

▶ Second, Canada's location on the Pacific Rim is another advantage for trade with Asia Pacific. Look at the map on page 31. You can see the Canadian port city of Vancouver is much closer to Tokyo than the American port of Los Angeles. What advantage does this give Canada over the U.S.?

▶ Finally, increased immigration to Canada from Asia Pacific countries, encouraged by Canada's official policy of multiculturalism, has also worked to Canada's economic advantage. Not only have these immigrants boosted local economies in many parts of Canada, they have also made it easier for Canada to establish trade ties with many Asia Pacific countries.

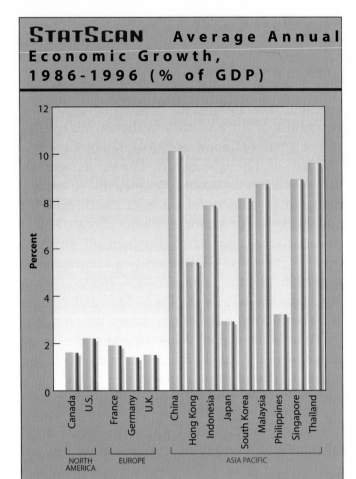

StatScan   Average Annual Economic Growth, 1986-1996 (% of GDP)

Source: World Bank

Figure 11-2 What does this graph show about the Asia Pacific region between 1986 and 1996? Does this graph help to answer the question in the chapter title? Explain.

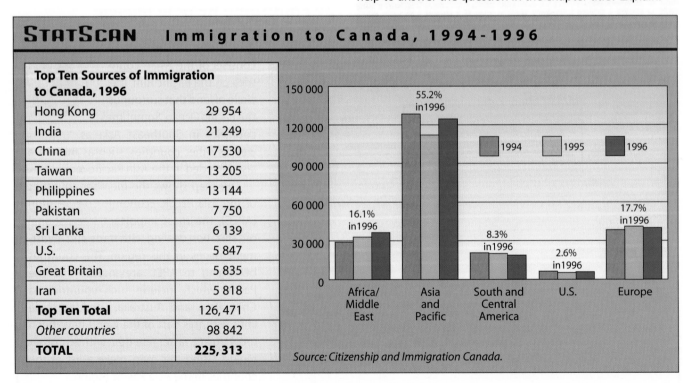

StatScan   Immigration to Canada, 1994-1996

Top Ten Sources of Immigration to Canada, 1996	
Hong Kong	29 954
India	21 249
China	17 530
Taiwan	13 205
Philippines	13 144
Pakistan	7 750
Sri Lanka	6 139
U.S.	5 847
Great Britain	5 835
Iran	5 818
Top Ten Total	**126,471**
Other countries	98 842
TOTAL	**225,313**

Source: Citizenship and Immigration Canada.

Figure 11-3 Immigrants from Asian countries made up 55.2% of all immigrants to Canada in 1996. What advantages would having Asian communities in major Canadian cities give Canada in its trade dealings with Asia Pacific countries?

Conflicts in Asia Pacific

As with any region that experiences great economic growth over a short period of time, the Asia Pacific region has its share of problems:

▶ Economic growth has not been shared equally. Some of the world's poorest countries are also located in the region. For example, Cambodia, torn apart by nearly 30 years of civil war, only has a per capita GNP of U.S. $200 and people's life expectancy is only 53 years.

▶ **Political repression** has been routinely practised by some governments which are controlled by powerful elites who enrich themselves at the expense of the people.

▶ Economic downturns can threaten countries which have undergone rapid economic change. For example, several of Asia Pacific's "economic wonders," such as Thailand, Indonesia, and South Korea were hit by a severe recession beginning in mid-1997. Because of economic interdependence in the region, through trade and investment, other countries such as Japan have been affected. Economists have compared these spreading economic problems to the Asian flu.

▶ Resource exploitation has also meant severe **environmental degradation** in some countries.

For example, between clear-cutting and forest fires, the rain forests on the island of Borneo are rapidly disappearing.

These problems together have created another—that of tension among countries in this region and their North American and European trading partners. The governments and their people in the Asia Pacific region resent being told what to do by Western nations and by powerful organizations such as the World Bank and the International Monetary Fund. See pages 80-82.

Figure 11-4 Civil unrest followed the economic downturn in Indonesia. Rioting by students became so widespread and violent that President Suharto was forced to resign in 1998 after 30 years in power.

CaseStudy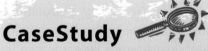

INDONESIA'S TROPICAL RAIN FORESTS

Huge forest fires, many set by farmers clearing land, occurred across the Indonesian islands in 1982, 1983, 1987, 1991, 1994, 1997, and 1998. Part of the blame can be put on population pressures on crowded Indonesian islands like Java which push people into the interior of sparsely populated areas such as Borneo in search of land. These farmers convert tropical rain forest into rice paddies and oil palm plantations. Fire is the popular choice to clear forests because it is cheap and fast. But with much of Borneo turned into a tinderbox by drought in the 1990s, many of these fires spread out of control. In 1998 these fires drove rare animal species from jungles and put tens of thousands of people in hospitals suffering from smoke inhalation.

Figure 11-5 A forest fire burns on Borneo island. Fires like this burned all over Borneo in 1998. In what way is Indonesia's drive for economic growth connected with rain forest loss in Borneo?

RECONNECT

1. What evidence can you cite to show that Asia Pacific countries are making a large impact on Canada's economy?

2. Why is Canada an attractive trading partner for Asia Pacific countries? Give two reasons and explain each of them.

FOCUS

This section will help you understand
    a. why Asian immigrants first came to Canada
    b. that Asian immigrants often faced racial discrimination.

The First Wave

Immigrants from Asia Pacific countries began to arrive on Canada's West Coast during the last half of the 19th century. Chinese immigrants made up the first wave. They were drawn to the gold rush that started in the Cariboo region of British Columbia in 1858. Although most of these settlers sought their fortunes by panning for gold along the Fraser River or in the Cariboo Mountains to the west of the Fraser, some set up businesses in Victoria. The next large group of Chinese immigrants arrived between 1880-84, when the Canadian Pacific Railway hired nearly 15 000 workers for the construction of the CPR through its most treacherous section, the mountains of British Columbia.

The first Japanese immigrant, a man named Mazano Nagano, arrived in British Columbia in 1877. He decided to leave his ship rather than return to Japan. By 1900, there were about 4000 Japanese working in the fishing industry along the B.C. coast. Like Nagano, many of them came from overcrowded fishing villages on the Japanese islands of Honshu and Kyushu. By 1914, about 10 000 Japanese had settled in Canada.

During the first decade of the 20th century, immigrants from the British colony of India entered Canada to work in B.C.'s many sawmills. About 5000 Indians, mostly Sikhs, came to Canada between 1905 and 1908. While Sikhs made up

Figure 12-1 Sikh immigrants from India working in a B.C. sawmill.

only a tiny percentage of the Indian population, they had become the backbone of the British colonial army. They came from a rich farming area in northern India known as the Punjab.

The first Sikh immigrants came to Canada after the 1902 coronation of King Edward VII in London. Sikh soldiers had made up most of the 1200 Indian colonial troops who attended this celebration of the British Empire. Sikh regiments from India and other British colonies travelled across Canada from Vancouver to Montreal to attend. Then they returned to Asia by retracing their journey across Canada. Many Sikh soldiers saw possibilities of improving their lives by immigrating to British Columbia.

StatScan	**Arrivals in Canada, Selected Years**					
Nationalities	**1906**	**1910**	**1920**	**1930**	**1940**	**1950**
Japanese	2996	429	526	218	44	11
Chinese	70	4667	1329	—	—	—
East Indian	2326	16	9	80	6	93

CONNECTIONS

THREE GENERATIONS

Grade 11 student Joanna Wong wrote the following essay as an entry in a competition organized by the Council for Canadian Unity. For her essay, Joanna won the $1000 first prize in the under-17 category. Here is a short excerpt from her essay.

In 1921 my grandfather immigrated to Gold Mountain, the name given to Canada by the Chinese people. He was chosen as the man "most likely to succeed" overseas. My grandfather's village pooled their resources to send him to Canada and raise the exorbitant $500 head tax needed to enter the country.

Honoured, my grandfather braved the arduous boat journey in search of prosperity for both himself and his family back in China. He was triumphant in this search and for 60 years ran a successful business and helped many others from his village seek a better life in the land of riches. He also raised nine children, the youngest of whom is my father.

Source: *The Vancouver Sun* (June 30, 1997), p. A11.

Figure 12-2   Joanna Wong and her father.

Figure 12-3   A Japanese Canadian boy wears a kilt to the 1920 unveiling of the Japanese Canadian war memorial located in Vancouver's Stanley Park. The memorial commemorated the Japanese Canadians who died fighting with the Canadian Expeditionary Force in Europe during World War I. Based on this photograph, would you say that the Japanese Canadian community had adapted to life in Canada by 1920? Explain your answer.

The Problem of Racial Discrimination

Once they arrived in Canada, immigrants from China, Japan, and India had to learn how to deal with the problem of racial discrimination. Lower wages for the same work, laws that discriminated, and outright violence were only three examples of this prejudice. More depressing in the long run, perhaps, was the day-to-day hostility that confronted anyone whose skin was not white.

Over the course of the 20th century, Asian Canadians gradually triumphed over racism and prejudice. The timeline on the next page provides a list of landmarks to show how Canadian society gradually changed over the first half of the 20th century in its attitude towards immigrants from Asia. The primary source shows just how serious the problem was in British Columbia at the turn of the century.

TIMELINE — Prejudice or Acceptance?

1885 — All Chinese immigrants are forced to pay a head tax of $50.

1900 — Wilfrid Laurier's Liberal government raises the Chinese head tax to $100.

1904 — The federal government increases the head tax on Chinese immigrants to $500, making it impossible for most Chinese men to bring their wives and children over from China. In the first year, the number of Chinese who pay the tax drops from 4719 to 8.

1907 — A mob of several hundred people riots, burning and looting stores in the Chinese and Japanese districts and beating any Asians they find on the street. Prime Minister Laurier calls for an investigation into the disturbance, and for compensation to be paid to all property owners who suffered damages.

1907 — The Canadian government passes an order-in-council requiring immigrants to travel to Canada on a "continuous journey" from their country of origin, and to possess at least $200. This meant that immigrants had to purchase a through-passage ticket from their home country to Canada. After this regulation came into effect, immigration from India fell from 2623 in 1907 to 6 in 1908.

1908 — Japan agrees with a Canadian request to limit the number of Japanese immigrants to Canada to 400 per year. The next year only 244 Japanese immigrants enter Canada.

1914 — The steamer *Komagata Maru*, with 376 Indian immigrants, is turned away from Vancouver harbour.

1923 — Canada passes the Chinese Exclusion Act, which bans all Chinese except students, merchants and diplomats from entering Canada. The act has the effect of virtually ending Chinese immigration to Canada.

1928 — Japan agrees to limit Japanese immigration to 150, including wives and children.
B.C.'s Liberal government petitions the federal government to end all Asian immigration and to repatriate as many Chinese and Japanese Canadians as possible.

1942 — All Japanese Canadians living in coastal areas of British Columbia are rounded up and sent to live in work camps in the interior of B.C. and Alberta.

1945 — The federal government uses the War Measures Act to deport up to 10 000 Japanese Canadians.

1947 — After a public outcry, the government revokes its 1945 orders-in-council after nearly 4000 Japanese Canadians were deported to Japan. Canada repeals the Chinese Exclusion Act of 1923. Chinese and Indian Canadians are granted the right to vote.

1949 — Japanese Canadians are granted the right to vote in Canadian federal elections. All restrictions on the movements of Japanese Canadians are repealed.

Primary Source
EARLY ATTITUDES TOWARD ASIA PACIFIC IMMIGRANTS

Here are some quotations that reveal racist attitudes which would be rejected by most Canadians today.

I think the fact that the Japanese is better qualified to adapt himself to the conditions prevailing here makes him a greater menace than the Chinaman to our own labour people.

—John Bowell, Methodist minister, in a statement to the *Royal Commission on Chinese and Japanese Immigration, 1902.*

We are all of the opinion that this province must be a white man's country… We do not wish to look forward to a day when our descendants will be dominated by Japanese, or Chinese, or any colour but their own… We are an outpost of the Empire, and that outpost we have to hold against all comers.

—From an editorial in the *Daily Province*, Vancouver, September 9, 1907.

The Chinese who are here usually congregate in one part of the city. The chief reason for this is companionship. Besides, the Chinese know that the white people have had no friendly feeling towards them for a number of years… This unfriendliness and want of respect… has not tended to induce them to abandon their own ways and modes of life.

—W. A. Cum Yow, born and raised in British Columbia, in a statement to the *Royal Commission on Chinese and Japanese Immigration, 1902.*

CaseStudy

THE *KOMAGATA MARU* INCIDENT

On May 23, 1914, a ship called the *Komagata Maru* sailed into Vancouver harbour, throwing the city and its officials into a turmoil that would last for the next two months. The ship carried 376 immigrants from India, most of them Sikhs. It had been chartered by a Sikh businessman who was determined to challenge the continuous journey regulation which made immigration from India nearly impossible. Since 1908, Indian immigrants had been kept out of Canada by a regulation that required them to arrive on a ship coming directly from India without stopping over anywhere else along the way. This continuous journey law had been challenged successfully in court, in 1913, by a group of 38 Sikhs who were then admitted to Canada. This encouraged other would-be immigrants to take a chance.

Local and federal government officials did everything in their power to prevent the passengers from leaving the ship, immediately placing it under a medical quarantine. Although the Sikh community in Vancouver rallied to the immigrants' cause, the government succeeded in cutting off new supplies of food and water to the ship. Vancouver's mayor organized a rally to insist that the passengers be denied entrance to the city.

Figure 12-4 How do you think these would-be immigrants felt after two months in Vancouver harbour?

In June the courts heard a test case for one of the Sikhs and upheld the government's order preventing the Sikh immigrants from landing. In all, 354 Sikhs hoping to immigrate to Canada spent two months in the heat of summer isolated on board the *Komagata Maru*. Only 22 passengers who were already residents of Canada were allowed to land. Finally, government officials called in the HMCS *Rainbow*, a Royal Canadian Navy cruiser, and forced the *Komagata Maru* out of Vancouver harbour and back across the Pacific.

Primary Source

THE ENEMY THAT NEVER WAS

On December 7, 1941, two years -and-two months after World War II began, the Japanese armed forces attacked the American naval base at Pearl Harbour in the Hawaiian Islands. Feelings against Japanese Canadians in B.C. quickly worsened, and in February 1942 nearly 21 000 Japanese Canadians were evacuated from coastal areas in B.C. Ken Adachi, author of an account of the evacuation called *The Enemy That Never Was*, as a child, was sent to an internment camp in the interior of B.C. Below are three selections from the book. What is the point of view expressed in the first two quotations below? Does the quotation from Prime Minister Mackenzie King support the title of Adachi's book? Explain.

Few regimes in modern history have imprisoned whole segments of society because of race. Nazi Germany is one of them; the Liberal government of Mackenzie King in Canada was another.
—Canadian author Timothy Findley, from the introduction he wrote to *The Enemy That Never Was, 1991*.

The dominant element in the development of the evacuation programme was racial prejudice, not a military estimate of a military problem. Some 21 000 persons were evacuated on a record which, as one commentator put it, "wouldn't support a conviction for stealing a dog."
—Ken Adachi, *The Enemy That Never Was, 1991*.

It is a fact that no person of Japanese race born in Canada has been charged with any act of sabotage or disloyalty during the years of the war.
—Prime Minister William Lyon Mackenzie King, quoted in *The Enemy That Never Was, 1991*.

RECONNECT

1. Why did the early immigrants from Asia Pacific come to Canada? Why did they remain in the face of the racial prejudice they experienced?

2. What indications were there that by 1950 the attitude of Canadian society as a whole toward immigrants from Asia Pacific was beginning to change for the better? Why do you think there was this gradual shift in public opinion?

FOCUS

This section will help you understand

a. to what extent immigration from Asia Pacific increased over the last half of the 20th century

b. the impact this increase in immigration from Asia Pacific has had on Canada.

Increasing Immigration from Asia Pacific

Immigration to Canada from the Asia Pacific region, which had been shut off for much of the first half of the 20th century, increased dramatically during the second half. This trend was so pronounced that by the end of the century, Asia Pacific has become the dominant source of immigrants to Canada. For example, in 1996 the largest number of immigrants to Canada came from seven Asian countries. At the top of the list was Hong Kong, followed in order by India, China, Taiwan, the Philippines, Pakistan, and Sri Lanka. According to the United Nations, in 1995 Asia contained approximately 60% of the world's total population. It is, therefore, home to the greatest number of potential immigrants to Canada of any region in the world.

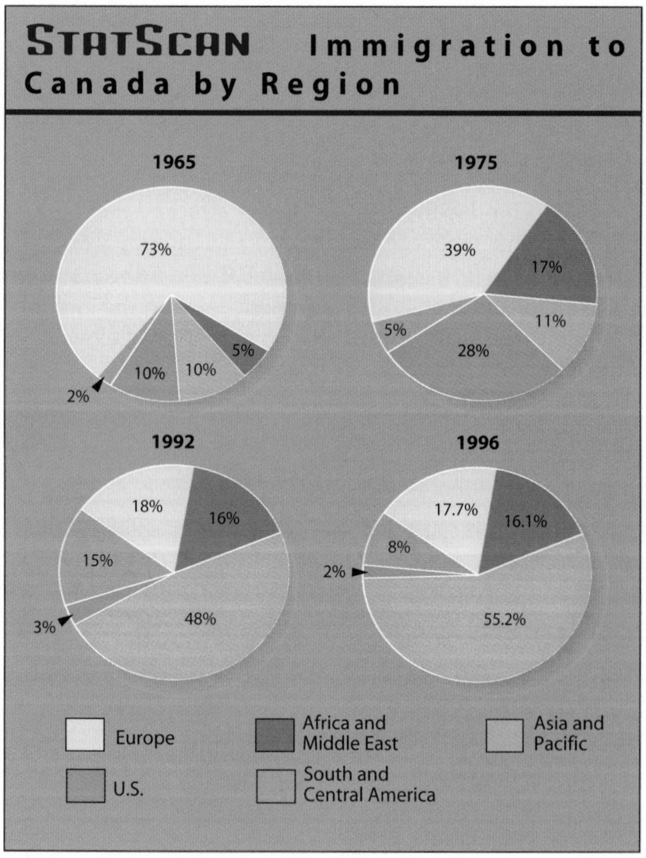

Immigrants from Asia Pacific countries provide Canada with important economic links to that region. In this sense it is fortunate that, as the economic clout of the Asia Pacific countries has grown, so has the number of immigrants it has sent to Canada. Why has immigration from this region been growing at such a sharp rate? Let's explore the reasons.

Push–Pull Factors

Immigrants come to Canada, as they do to any country, for a variety of reasons. **Demographers** speak of migration in terms of push–pull factors. People are attracted to a new country by "pull" factors. An example of this is a business person who is "pulled" to Canada by an investment opportunity. Under current immigration laws, the Canadian government classifies such an investor as a business immigrant and gives this person preferential treatment when he or she is applying to live in Canada. The government assumes that anyone who invests a large amount of money in Canada will create jobs. This, in turn, should have a beneficial effect on the economy.

At the other end of the spectrum are refugees from war-torn countries in Southeast Asia such as Cambodia. These people are "pushed" out of their homeland by the violence of war. They see Canada as a stable country in which to start a new life. Many immigrants arrive in Canada because of a combination of push–pull factors.

StatScan Immigration to Canada by Region

1965
- 73%
- 10%
- 10%
- 5%
- 2%

1975
- 39%
- 17%
- 11%
- 28%
- 5%

1992
- 18%
- 16%
- 15%
- 48%
- 3%

1996
- 17.7%
- 16.1%
- 8%
- 55.2%
- 2%

- ☐ Europe
- ☐ U.S.
- ☐ Africa and Middle East
- ☐ South and Central America
- ☐ Asia and Pacific

Figure 13-1 These graphs show how drastically changes to Canadian immigration laws and the official policy of multiculturalism have opened up new sources of immigration to this country. Which region has experienced the greatest increase since 1965? Which has experienced the greatest decrease?

Impact of Immigration from Asia Pacific

For many people the issue of immigration raises a number of difficult questions. One of the hardest to answer is this: What kind of Canada do Canadians want? This debate has grown louder and more spirited since 1980 as the sources of immigration have shifted to Asia and away from Europe and the U.S. There are at least three "sides" to the current debate.

▶ Critics of the present immigration policy argue that the increase in the number of immigrants from Asia Pacific countries will eventually change Canada's population base so that it will no longer be mainly European (that is British and French). They say this will change the traditional foundation of the Canadian identity. This is one of the arguments that greeted the original immigrants from Asia Pacific more than 100 years ago.

▶ Supporters of current policies assert that Asian immigrants have made important contributions to the culture and economic well-being of Canada. Immigrants not only enrich Canada's cultural mix, they say, but also inject money into the economy by starting businesses and buying houses.

▶ A third group feels that immigration should be regulated by the economy. When the economy is

Figure 13-2 This photo was taken in a high school in B.C. How does this picture mirror the graphs on page 38?

booming, more immigration should be encouraged because more jobs are available. In times of recession, however, immigration should be discouraged because there are not enough jobs for the people who are already here.

Regardless of these different opinions, there can be little doubt that immigration from Asia Pacific has already changed the face of Canada.

NewsFlash

In Toronto, Minorities set to be majority

By Elaine Carey

In less than 18 months, the majority of people in the new city of Toronto will be non-white, according to a new report.

Toronto is the most ethnically diverse city in the world, the report says, and does far more than any other to help that mix cope.

The centre [Toronto's Access and Equity Centre] analyzed data from the 1996 census, separating Toronto from the 905 area, and found:

• By the year 2000, visible minorities will make up 54 per cent of the population of Toronto, up from 30 per cent in 1991 and only 3 per cent in 1961.

• Toronto is home to 42% of the total non-white population in Canada, including almost half the South Asian and black population, as well as two-fifths of the Chinese, Koreans and Filipino.

• Over 70 000 immigrants come to Toronto every year. Immigrants come from 169 countries, speaking 100

different languages and 42 per cent speak neither English nor French when they arrive.

• One in five Toronto residents arrived in Canada after 1981 and one in 10 came after 1991. The population of immigrants grew at four times the rate of the non-immigrant between 1991 and 1996.

• The largest concentration of immigrants is found in the North York, Scarborough and Toronto community council areas, accounting for three-quarters of the total.

• About one-third of Toronto's residents neither speak English nor French at home and the top three languages are Chinese in many dialects, Italian and Portuguese.

Despite the problems, "there is nowhere in the world where diversity works as well as it does here," Mayor Mel Lastman said in an interview. "The more we talk about it, the better it will be for everyone."

Source: *The Toronto Star* (June 7, 1998) p. A1.

BIOGRAPHY

Subject: Herb Dhaliwal, Minister of Revenue

Dates: Born, 1952

Most Notable Accomplishment: Herb Dhaliwal is the first Indo-Canadian to become a minister in the federal Cabinet. As minister of revenue, he is one of only three Cabinet ministers in the history of Canada to have come from a visible minority.

Figure 13-3 Herb Dhaliwal.

Thumbnail Sketch: Herb Dhaliwal was born in the Punjab in India and emigrated to Canada with his parents when he was five years old. As a student at the University of British Columbia, he started a janitorial service in the basement of his parents' home. This first business venture grew into airport limousine and real estate companies that, by the late 1990s, employed about 500 people across Canada. A self-made millionaire, Dhaliwal was first elected to Parliament in 1993 as a Liberal from the riding of Burnaby South in B.C. He was one of the first two Sikhs elected to Parliament. After his re-election in 1997, Dhaliwal was appointed to Cabinet by Prime Minister Jean Chrétien.

Significant Quote: "Canada has changed in the past 15 years ... but most of our institutions don't reflect that change. One of the things I can do is make changes that put the new face of Canada into our institutions. We've always had this idea that Canada is just French and English, but we have a multicultural society."

CaseStudy

IMMIGRATION AND GOVERNMENT POLICY

During the last decades of the 20th century immigration probably has had a greater impact on Canada than almost any other country in the world. Canada accepts nearly 1 million immigrants and refugees every four years (about 224 000 in 1996). This is by far the highest per capita rate of immigration in the world. Immigrants already account for one in six of Canada's total population and one in four of Ontario's population.

The Immigration Act

Immigrants and refugees to Canada are governed by the Immigration Act of 1976. Because the Canadian government felt a loophole in the law allowed too many immigrants to claim refugee status, the Immigration Act was changed in 1992. The law also

Figure 13-4   Minister of Immigration Lucienne Robillard.

requires the minister of immigration to submit an immigration plan every year by November 1. This plan shows the number of immigrants in four main categories who can enter Canada during the next calendar year. The immigration plan is debated in the House of Commons and members of the public can also voice their opinions. Because Canada is a popular destination for immigrants, the number of people wanting to come to Canada is much greater than in the annual immigration plan.

Since the Immigration Act was passed in 1976, Canadian immigration regulations do not discriminate on the grounds of race, country of origin, sex, or religion. The Act does, however, allow quicker entry of the immediate family members of Canadian citizens as well as established business people who are willing to invest a certain amount in Canada. In 1997, this amount rose from $350 thousand to $450 thousand depending on the province.

The Impact of Immigration in the 1990s

In response to the rise in immigration, public opinions polls indicate that many Canadians feel immigration levels are too high. For example, in July 1996 an Angus Reid poll found that when asked if immigrant numbers were appropriate, 44% of Canadians responded too many immigrants were coming to Canada.

As a result of public opinion, Immigration Minister Lucienne Robillard announced in November 1996 that immigration levels would remain the same for 1997 at 220 000. This trend has continued. The target immigration levels for 1998 was between 200 000 and 225 000 immigrants.

Since the eight largest sources of Canadian immigration are non-white countries, immigration is often bound up in issues of race and ethnicity. For this reason the federal government has approached the issue of immigration cautiously. In 1998, the federal government issued a series of recommendations which would change some aspects of immigration policy.

StatScan Immigration to Canada, 1900-1996

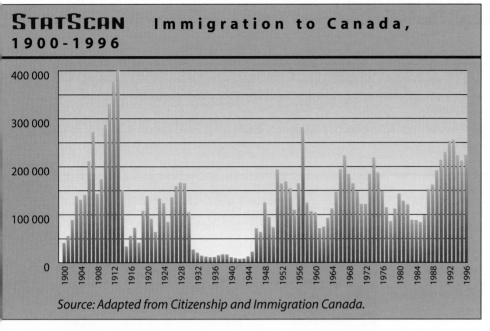

Source: Adapted from Citizenship and Immigration Canada.

Figure 13-5 When were the highest levels of immigration? When were the lowest? Explain. Describe immigration to Canada during the last 20 years.

Immigration and Multiculturalism

In 1971, Prime Minister Pierre Trudeau proclaimed **multiculturalism** an official government policy. This policy means that the Canadian government is committed to recognizing and promoting the different cultural groups that live in Canada, not just the "dominant" and traditional cultures of the English and French. Since the passage of the 1976 Immigration Act, Canadian government policy on immigration has been guided by the concept of multiculturalism. This has meant that the percentage of immigrants from areas such as Asia Pacific, Africa, the Middle East, and South America has increased sharply, while it has declined from Europe and the U.S.

CROSSFIRE

IS MULTICULTURALISM BENEFICIAL TO CANADA?

No

Multiculturalism...has heightened our differences rather than diminished them; it has preached tolerance rather than encouraging acceptance; and it is leading us into a divisiveness so entrenched that we face a future of multiple solitudes with no central notion to bind us.

—Neil Bissoondath, *Selling Illusions: The Cult of Multiculturalism in Canada* (Toronto: Penguin, 1994), p. 192.

Yes

Multiculturalism in the 1990s is about removing barriers to the full participation, full contribution and full citizenship of all Canadians, regardless of their background and cultural heritage. Its policies are aimed at breaking down the barriers to equal rights and responsibilities—barriers such as racism, low literacy levels and disregard for the rights of minorities.

—Canadian Senator Donald H. Oliver, *The Montreal Gazette* (September 1, 1996), p. A6.

Figure 13-6 Canadian writer Neil Bissoondath.

Figure 13-7 Canadian Senator Donald H. Oliver.

RECONNECT

1. In what ways has the pattern of immigration to Canada changed in the last 50 years?

2. What is the connection in Canada between multiculturalism and immigration? Explain.

3. Reread the Crossfire box to determine which opinion about multiculturalism you agree with most. Write a one-paragraph statement explaining your view.

FOCUS

This section will help you understand
a. why Great Britain returned Hong Kong to the People's Republic of China
b. how this event affected Canada.

Economic Links Between Canada and Hong Kong

The sprawling port city of Hong Kong is officially called a Special Administrative Region of China. Before 1997, Hong Kong belonged to Great Britain, and under British rule developed into the world's largest **container port** and a great financial and manufacturing centre. Britain had only leased Hong Kong from China, however, promising that it would be returned by the end of the 20th century. In 1984, the two countries signed an agreement stating the transition would take place in 1997.

Over the second half of the 20th century, Canada and Hong Kong developed a strong economic relationship for two reasons:

▶ First, Hong Kong is a manufacturing centre with few natural resources, while Canada's economic

Figure 14-1 Hong Kong harbour is the largest container port in the world. In 1995, Hong Kong was Canada's tenth largest trading partner, while Canada was Hong Kong's eighth largest. Hong Kong is also a large investor in Canada. In 1995, it invested $3 billion in Canada, which accounted for 27% of all Asian investment.

MAP STUDY

HONG KONG: A SPECIAL ADMINISTRATIVE REGION OF CHINA

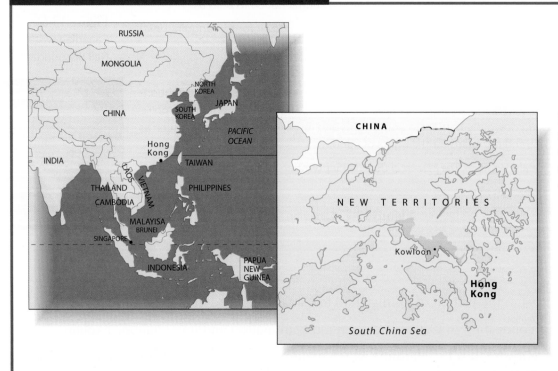

By examining these maps, can you tell why Hong Kong is well situated for world trade? Explain.

strength rests on its great reserves of natural resources. Hong Kong imports resources such as lumber, minerals, and fish, while exporting to Canada products of high technology. Hong Kong and Canada both have an association with Great Britain as well. Because English is one of Hong Kong's official languages, it is easier for Canadians to do business there than in many places in Asia Pacific.

▶ Second, the political uncertainty surrounding Great Britain's return of Hong Kong to China in 1997 meant that many people in Hong Kong immigrated to Canada looking for a quiet, friendly place to live. Great Britain had fostered a capitalist economy in Hong Kong, and the city had grown to become one of the busiest financial centres in the world. China, on the other hand, has a communist economy. Some business people in Hong Kong feared that China would reform the economy so that engaging in private business would become more difficult, if not impossible.

StatScan Hong Kong–Canada Trade, 1991-1996

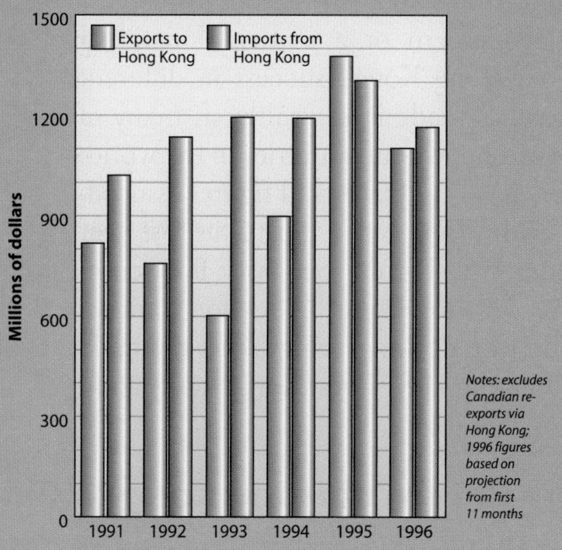

Notes: excludes Canadian re-exports via Hong Kong; 1996 figures based on projection from first 11 months

Source: Department of Foreign Affairs and International Trade Canada

Figure 14-2 This graph shows the dollar value of trade between Hong Kong and Canada from 1991 to 1996. Which country usually has a trade surplus? What happened in 1995? Does the trade relationship seem to be one between equals? Explain.

TIMELINE  Hong Kong

1839-42 The first Opium War. When China prohibits imports of opium from British India, Britain declares war. By the Treaty of Nanking in 1842, China cedes Hong Kong Island to Britain. Britain begins to develop Hong Kong's harbour, which is very deep and can be entered either from the east or the west. It also lies on the main trade routes of the Asia Pacific region.

1856-60 The second Opium War. France joins Britain against China, when China again tries to restrict the sale of opium. At the end of the war in 1860, China cedes the southern part of the Kowloon Peninsula and Stonecutter's Island to Britain.

1898 China leases the New Territories and 235 surrounding islands to Great Britain for a period of 99 years. The population of Hong Kong swells to about 300 000 by the turn of the century, and it becomes a major transition point for trade between China and European countries.

1941 The population of Hong Kong reaches 1.6 million, as refugees flee mainland China before advancing Japanese armies. On Christmas day, Japanese troops crush British and Canadian defenders and occupy Hong Kong for the rest of World War II.

1945 Under the Japanese occupation, the economy stagnates and the population falls to about 650 000 by the end of the war. British troops re-enter the city on August 30, 1945.

1950 At the start of the Korean War, the United Nations places an embargo on trade with China and North Korea. This does serious damage to Hong Kong's economy. In response, Hong Kong develops its manufacturing industries, concentrating especially on textiles and clothing.

1967 The Cultural Revolution in China. Major riots break out in Hong Kong as workers protest against low wages and frightful working conditions.

1984 China and Great Britain sign a joint declaration that arranges for the return of all the Hong Kong territories to China in 1997. China guarantees that the Hong Kong Special Administrative Region will not have to change its economic and social systems for at least 50 years.

1989 The Tiananmen Square massacre in Beijing. Chinese troops fire on students advocating democratic reforms.

1997 On July 1, Great Britain formally hands Hong Kong back to China.

Hong Kong's Wealth

Why was China so eager to regain control of Hong Kong? It was not just a territorial concern or a matter of national pride. Hong Kong's success in different areas has made it as wealthy as many of the most powerful countries in the world. Here is a list of facts and figures associated with Hong Kong during its last year under British rule. See how they compare with the same figures for Canada. Why would Hong Kong be so desirable to China? How does Hong Kong compare to Canada?

Hong Kong and Canada, 1996		
	Hong Kong	**Canada**
Population	6.3 million	30.3 million (1997)
Area	1095 sq. km	9 970 610 sq. km
Gross national product (GNP)	$153 billion	$569.9 billion
GNP world rank	26	9
GNP per capita	$24 290	$19 020
GNP per capita world rank	13	18
Unemployment	2.4%	9.7%

Dollar amounts are in U.S. dollars.

Source: World Bank.

The Return of Hong Kong to China

Britain's return of Hong Kong to China has had an impact on Canadian immigration rates. Wealthy residents of Hong Kong began to immigrate to Canada in large numbers in 1985, the year after Britain signed an agreement formalizing the terms of the colony's return to China. People in Hong Kong were worried that their capitalist economy and their democratic form of government might be outlawed when China took over. This fear grew into panic after the Tiananmen Square massacre, when Chinese troops crushed a pro-democracy demonstration.

The destination of choice for more than half of the Hong Kong émigrés was Canada. In fact, since 1987, Hong Kong has been the largest single source for Canadian immigrants. Between 1987 and 1996, more than 290 000 immigrants arrived in Canada from Hong Kong. This represented 13% of all Canadian immigrants over that 10-year period.

As the date of Hong Kong's return to China approached, and circumstances seemed less threatening, some of the Hong Kongers who had emigrated and become Canadian citizens decided to return to Hong Kong. At present, Canadian citizens make up one of the largest minority groups in Hong Kong, numbering about 150 000. Often those who returned to Hong Kong left family members, especially children attending school, behind in Canada. This two-way flow of people has given Canada a unique business window on China and on the rest of the Asia Pacific region as well.

Figure 14-3 Great Britain returns Hong Kong to China.

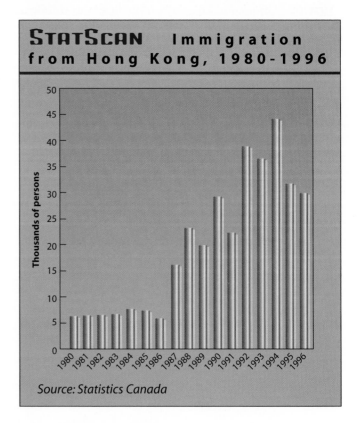

StatScan Immigration from Hong Kong, 1980-1996

Source: Statistics Canada

Figure 14-4 Immigration to Canada from Hong Kong rose steadily during the period 1980 to 1996. What events do you think caused the sharpest rises in the number of immigrants?

The Impact of Hong Kong Immigrants on Canada

Citizenship and Immigration Canada places all immigrants to Canada into different categories. About 25% of all immigrants from Hong Kong fall into the business category. This is a very high percentage when compared with emigrants from other countries to Canada, which average about 6% business immigrants.

Such a high percentage of business immigrants means that Hong Kongers have had a strong impact on the Canadian economy as a whole, especially in British Columbia and Ontario. Here is a list of some significant accomplishments by Hong Kong immigrants to Canada.

▶ Hong Kong philanthropists have donated millions of dollars to the University of British Columbia which has expanded the academic facilities. Four of the most generous donations have involved the following buildings and programs:

  - The Chan Centre for the Performing Arts.
  - The Sing Tao School for Journalism.
  - The C.K. Choi Building of the Institute of Asian Research.
  - The David Lam Management Research Library.

▶ Simon Fraser University has also benefited from the generosity of the Hong Kong community in B.C. In 1990, the David Lam Centre for International Communication opened there after receiving a $1 million donation from Lam, a former B.C. lieutenant-governor.

▶ Hong Kong movie director Jackie Chan filmed *Rumble in the Bronx* in Vancouver, which was estimated to have pumped millions into the local economy. Many other films and TV shows by Hong Kong artists are filmed in and around Vancouver.

▶ Hong Kong entrepreneurs have been active in major real estate developments in Canada, including:

  - Li Ka-shing's $3 billion development of 82.5 hectares in downtown Vancouver which started with his purchase of the Canada Expo lands in 1988.
  - Terry Hui and Victor Li's billion-dollar development of 18.2 hectares near the Skydome in downtown Toronto which will include up to 6000 highrise condominium units and townhouse units. The total cost will run into several $100 millions.
  - Eight Asian malls built by Hong Kong immigrants in Richmond, B.C.

▶ Hong Kongers have also made their mark on Canadian politics. Canadian politicians of Hong Kong descent include:

  - Jenny Kwan and Ida Chong, elected as MLAs in the B.C. legislature.
  - Raymond Chan and Sophia Leung, elected to the federal Parliament in 1997.
  - David Lam, served as lieutenant-governor of B.C. from 1988 to 1995.

Figure 14-5 Former B.C. Lieutenant-Governor and successful real estate developer David Lam who immigrated to Canada in 1967. "Canada isn't a racist society," Lam once said. "Instead it is a wonderfully varied, multi-ethnic, very caring and compassionate society. That is why I tell Hong Kong people who immigrate to Canada: Give money to charity and donate it to schools and other worthwhile things in Canadian society."

RECONNECT

1. Why did Great Britain have to return Hong Kong to China? Explain fully.

2. Why did the return of Hong Kong to China have such a strong impact on the rates of Hong Kong immigration to Canada?

3. What contributions are immigrants from Hong Kong making to Canadian society?

The Benefits of Asia Pacific Trade

Trade, the buying and selling of goods and services between nations, has become vital to the Canadian economy. In 1997, Canada was the seventh-largest trading country in the world. During the last decades of the 20th century Canadian trade with Asia Pacific increased at a faster rate than with any other region in the world. Asia Pacific countries contain 60% of the world's population, and form the largest economic market in the world. To sustain the health of its own economy, Canada has to develop strong trade ties with Asia Pacific.

Not surprisingly, most of Canada's Asia Pacific trade is conducted through the province of British Columbia. As well, B.C.'s resource industries are dependent on markets in Asia Pacific, especially Japan. When the economies of Asia Pacific countries are doing well, economists have noted that trade across the Pacific Ocean has helped B.C. to withstand some of the recessions experienced by other Canadian provinces.

M A P S T U D Y **CANADIAN TRADE WITH ASIA PACIFIC, 1997**

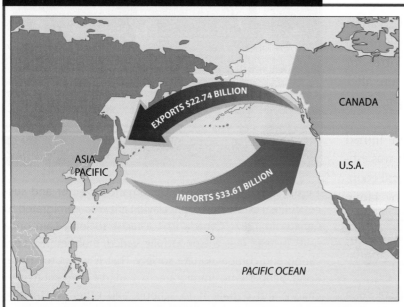

The arrows show the dollar amounts of trade between Canada and Asia Pacific in 1997. Does Canada have more imports or exports with the Asia Pacific region? How would you describe Canada's balance of trade with Asia Pacific?

Traditionally, most Canadian exports to Asia Pacific have come from resource industries such as mining, forestry, and agriculture. Recently, Canadian exports have expanded into other areas such as telecommunications, power generation, environmental technology, and management services. Asia Pacific exports to Canada are dominated by automobiles, electronic equipment such as televisions, radios, and CD players, and high-tech items like computer chips.

Canadian Exports to Asia Pacific, 1997 *(Canadian dollars)*		Canadian Imports from Asia Pacific, 1997 *(Canadian dollars)*	
Minerals	$3 592 000 000	Electronic/Electrical Products	$8 072 608 000
Wood Products	$3 048 000 000	Computers/Peripheral Equipment	$3 442 579 000
Metals	$1 860 000 000	Motor Vehicles	$2 700 211 000
Pulp	$1 803 961 000	Machinery (except electrical)	$2 403 000 000
Chemicals	$1 712 000 000	Clothing	$2 005 000 000
Electronic/Electrical Products	$1 546 000 000	Motor Vehicle Parts	$1 712 000 000
Wheat	$1 205 819 000	TVs/CD Players/Radios	$1 144 813 000
Oilseed	$983 576 000	Toys	$949 949 000
Transportation Products	$905 858 000	Shoes	$686 074 000
Meat Products	$857 248 000	Other	$10 499 380 000
Machinery (except electrical)	$772 391 000	**TOTAL**	**$33 615 614 000**
Fish	$663875 000		
Newsprint	$629 819 000		
Other	$3 167 992 000		
TOTAL	**$22 749 539 000**		

CaseStudy

TEAM CANADA

As trade with Asia Pacific increased during the 1980s and 1990s, the Canadian government began to take an active role in strengthening economic ties with the region. These special efforts were considered necessary because in Asia Pacific it is traditional for business contracts to be signed only after long-term relationships have been developed.

Prime Minister Jean Chrétien led three special tours to specific areas in Asia Pacific to encourage more trade. For these tours, the prime minister created a group called Team Canada, which consisted of political leaders (usually provincial premiers and the mayors of larger Canadian cities) and about 300 business leaders from different industries. Including the prime minister as well as provincial premiers was intended to show Asia Pacific countries that Canada was a stable and secure place to do business. For each trip, Team Canada chartered a jet to take it to cities where meetings were arranged with local business and political leaders. The three trips and some of their results are listed below.

Figure 15-1 Team Canada in 1997 in Seoul, South Korea. What was the purpose of including political leaders in Team Canada? Do you think these kinds of visits are a good idea or not? Explain.

China—1994

The first Team Canada trip was to China and consisted of Prime Minister Chrétien, nine premiers, and 400 business people. The 14-day trip resulted in signed contracts worth $9 billion. The largest contract was for the sale of two CANDU nuclear reactors worth $3.5 billion.

India, Pakistan, and Malaysia—1996

The next Team Canada trip was to India, Pakistan, and Malaysia. Prime Minister Chrétien was joined on the 12-day trip by seven premiers and 300 business people. Contracts worth $8.7 billion were signed. Craig Kielburger of Free the Children gained national attention when he met with Prime Minister Chrétien in India to talk about the exploitation of children in countries around the world.

South Korea, Philippines, and Thailand—1997

The third Team Canada trip made stops in South Korea, the Philippines, and Thailand. Nine premiers and 450 business people joined Prime Minister Chrétien for the 12-day trip which resulted in $2.1 billion worth of contracts for Canadian companies.

Primary Source

"CANADA IS STILL A TIMID PLAYER IN ASIA"

Today (1996), you can find Canadians in every part of Asia—building houses or delivering software and executive jets to Japan, constructing nuclear power plants in Korea, installing phone systems and even building hockey rinks in China, running law offices, banks and insurance companies in Hong Kong, operating mines in Indonesia, managing engineering and construction projects in Singapore, designing transit systems in Malaysia and helping install telecommunications networks in Thailand.

Yet, despite this activity, Canada is still a timid player in Asia, much more active than it was a decade ago but still far from realizing the region's potential.

…These same countries are also investing heavily in knowledge and ideas. The Japanese government for example, just approved a plan to increase public spending on science and technology by 50 per cent over the next 5 years, to nearly $215 billion.

…It would be foolish to simply extrapolate Asia's recent success indefinitely into the future. There are many things that could go wrong.

…But something clearly is happening in Asia…It's growing and modernizing…In the process of changing itself, Asia will change the entire world.

Which is why 1997, the Year of Asia Pacific in Canada, deserves to be taken seriously…

—David Crane, *The Toronto Star* (July 26, 1996), p. A15.

Figure 15-2 How does this cartoon illustrate what *The Toronto Star's* David Crane is saying in his article? "The Rim" refers to the Pacific Rim, the circle of countries that surrounds the Pacific Ocean and includes the Asia Pacific region. What does the beaver represent?

CaseStudy

TRADE AND THE
EXPLOITATION OF CHILDREN

A remarkable Canadian teenager, Craig Kielburger, is making a tremendous contribution towards ending the exploitation of children in the Third World. In 1995, Kielburger founded an organization, called Free the Children, which is dedicated to stopping the exploitation of children around the world. Free the Children and Kielburger have taken on many issues ranging from indentured children to child prostitution. Kielburger travels the globe speaking out against the abuses children face with such insight and conviction that veteran politicians are often moved to take action.

In January 1996, the gutsy 13 year old travelled to several Asian countries to find out more about the working and living conditions of child labourers. While in India, he met with Prime Minister Chrétien and other members of the Team Canada trade mission to India. He convinced the Canadian government to fund programs to help exploited children as part of its foreign aid program. As well, he made Canadian business people aware that they also had a responsibility to ensure the contracts they signed did not involve taking advantage of child labourers in the countries they were visiting.

Figure 15-3 Craig Kielburger in India, 1996. Later in the year, speaking to top executives from major American corporations, he asserted: "We just do not believe that the adults of the world can put a man on the moon and invent nuclear bombs, but cannot feed the world's children."

Drawbacks of Trade with Asia Pacific

As you can see on the map on page 46, Canada has a trade deficit with the Asia Pacific region. This means that Canada imports more from the region than it exports to it. Asia Pacific, on the other hand, has a **trade surplus** with Canada. Canada's economy can suffer from a trade deficit since Canada, as a whole, is buying more goods than it is selling. A trade deficit can lead to more debt as well as, in the long run, higher unemployment.

Since Canada trades so heavily with Asia Pacific, many Canadian jobs depend on the continued health of this trading relationship. A large part of Canada's exports to Asia Pacific consist of raw materials and semi-processed goods, which are cheaper to produce than the manufactured goods it imports from the region. Fewer workers are needed to extract raw materials than to produce manufactured goods. In this respect, the heavy reliance in Canada on exports of natural resources means there are fewer jobs for Canadian workers.

Asia Pacific trade also has a negative impact on Canadian employment rates for another reason. The manufactured goods that Canada imports from Asia Pacific countries like Malaysia are often produced by workers earning

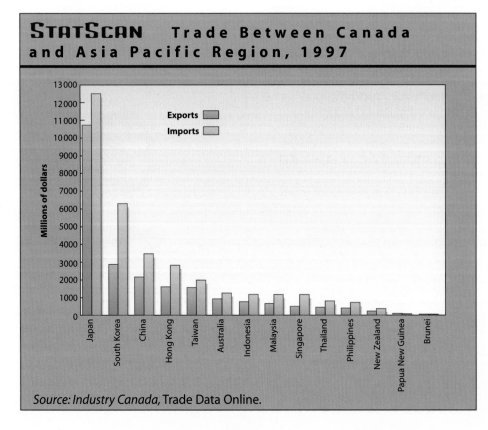

StatScan Trade Between Canada and Asia Pacific Region, 1997

Source: Industry Canada, Trade Data Online.

Figure 15-4 Examine this graph. Which country is far and away Canada's largest trading partner in the Asia Pacific? With which countries does Canada have a trade surplus? With which countries does Canada have a trade deficit? Explain.

much lower wages than they would in Canada. In Japan, where factory workers are well paid, mechanical robots have replaced human workers on many assembly lines. Poorly paid workers and efficient robots make it difficult for Canadian factories to compete against their rivals in Asia Pacific. Some Canadian factories have had to close and others to relocate to Asia Pacific countries. Both these trends have cost a number of Canadian workers their jobs.

APEC and Canada

The Asia-Pacific Economic Co-operation (APEC) is an organization of 21 Asia Pacific countries including Canada. It was founded in 1989 to encourage stronger trade ties between its members. Considered as a unit, APEC countries account for 50% of the total output of goods in the world. Although the member countries have widely different cultures and systems of government, they all see the advantages of working together to improve their economies. For this reason, APEC is a good example of the increasing interdependence among countries in this region.

Canada has taken an active role in APEC since its founding. In 1997, Vancouver hosted APEC's annual meeting, which was attended by the leaders of the member countries. At this meeting the leaders agreed to eliminate tariffs among their countries by the year 2010. By pulling down all tariff barriers, APEC countries hope to expand trade opportunities.

Figure 15-5 An electronics plant in China. Why can so many goods be manufactured more cheaply in Asia than in Canada?

Figure 15-6 Prime Minister Chrétien chaired the 1997 APEC meeting in Vancouver. "APEC is extremely important," he said, "because the money, the people, the growth, and the dollars of tomorrow will be in the Pacific. For Canada, our trade with the Pacific is bigger than our trade with the European continent by 50%."

Figure 15-7 Not everybody agrees with APEC's aims. During the APEC conference in Vancouver, thousands of people protested against human rights abuses in China and Indonesia, and accused APEC leaders of worsening conditions for low paid labourers in Asia Pacific countries. A storm of controversy followed when protestors were tear-gassed and arrested by the RCMP.

RECONNECT

1. Why is trade with Asia Pacific so important to the Canadian economy?

2. Describe at least two steps Canada has taken to expand trade with Asia Pacific. Are these steps adequate or not? Support your answer.

3. What is a trade deficit? Why does Canada have a trade deficit with Asia Pacific?

> **FOCUS**
>
> This section will help you understand
> a. that Japan has developed one of the strongest economies in the world
> b. that Japan is Canada's most important source of foreign investment from Asia Pacific
> c. that this foreign investment has had positive and negative effects on Canada.

Japanese Investment in Canada

After the U.S. and Britain, Japan has become the largest foreign investor in Canada. Japan is also Canada's second largest trading partner in the world. Of the countries in the Asia Pacific, Japan invests nearly three times more in Canada than Hong Kong—the second highest investor in the region. Japan has invested in many sectors of the Canadian economy:

► *Automobiles.* By 1989 three of the largest Japanese auto makers had built car assembly plants in southern Ontario with a total manufac-

turing capacity of 370 000 cars per year. By 1998, Honda, Toyota, and Suzuki had increased their investments in manufacturing plants to $3.7 billion. When the planned expansions are complete, Japanese auto makers will be able to manufacture 730 000 motor vehicles in Canada. The number of Canadian workers will reach 8000 at these plants. When other workers in Japanese car parts manufacturing as well as at car dealerships across Canada are added, the total workforce will be over 40 000.

M a p S t u d y — JAPANESE AUTOMOBILE PLANTS IN ONTARIO

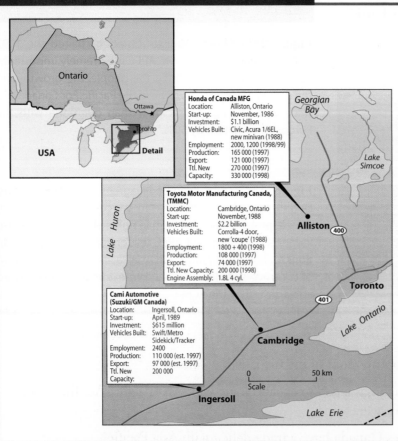

Honda of Canada MFG
Location:	Alliston, Ontario
Start-up:	November, 1986
Investment:	$1.1 billion
Vehicles Built:	Civic, Acura 1/6EL, new minivan (1988)
Employment:	2000, 1200 (1998/99)
Production:	165 000 (1997)
Export:	121 000 (1997)
Ttl. New	270 000 (1997)
Capacity:	330 000 (1998)

Toyota Motor Manufacturing Canada, (TMMC)
Location:	Cambridge, Ontario
Start-up:	November, 1988
Investment:	$2.2 billion
Vehicles Built:	Corrolla-4 door, new 'coupe' (1988)
Employment:	1800 + 400 (1998)
Production:	108 000 (1997)
Export:	74 000 (1997)
Ttl. New Capacity:	200 000 (1998)
Engine Assembly:	1.8L 4 cyl.

Cami Automotive (Suzuki/GM Canada)
Location:	Ingersoll, Ontario
Start-up:	April, 1989
Investment:	$615 million
Vehicles Built:	Swift/Metro Sidekick/Tracker
Employment:	2400
Production:	110 000 (est. 1997)
Export:	97 000 (est. 1997)
Ttl. New Capacity:	200 000

In 1996 about 80% of the motor vehicles produced at these plants were exported, mostly to the U.S. From 1992 to 1996 Canada exported more Japanese vehicles than it imported which has helped Canada's **balance of trade.** In 1996 Canadian exports of Japanese vehicles nearly doubled imports from Japan, the U.S., and Mexico combined.

The main attraction to Canada for Japanese auto makers is access to the North American market, especially the U.S. Under the North American Free Trade Agreement, Japanese cars produced in Canada qualify for tariff-free entry to the U.S. if 75% of the cost comes from Canadian-based manufacturing. This has encouraged more Japanese investment in auto parts plants so that Canadian-made cars qualify under NAFTA regulations.

▶ *Resource Industries.* Japanese companies have invested heavily in resource industries, especially in forestry and mining in B.C. and Alberta. For example, the Japanese-owned Daishowa Inc. has constructed a number of pulp and paper mills in the Peace River region of Alberta worth over $1 billion.

▶ *Real Estate.* Japanese investors have acquired and also built hotels in Canadian cities and resort destinations. Some major five star hotels with Japanese owners are the Pan Pacific in Vancouver, the Chateau Whistler in Whistler, B.C., and the Banff Springs Hotel in Banff, Alberta.

▶ *Tourism.* Japan is the source of the largest number of visitors to Canada after the U.S. and Britain. In 1997, approximately 600 000 Japanese visitors spent about $640 million in Canada. The Japanese spend more per person in Canada than visitors from any other country.

These Japanese investments have helped to build up the Canadian economy and to provide thousands of jobs. On the other hand, some of these investments have been criticized. Examine the map study and case study for specific information on two kinds of Japanese investments.

CaseStudy

SELLING CANADA'S FORESTS

Perhaps the most widely criticized example of Asia Pacific investment in Canada is the huge Japanese investment in the Canadian forestry industry. Japan for many years has been unable to satisfy its own demand for paper, which is made from pulp wood. Japan simply cannot harvest enough trees from its own forests to supply the pulp necessary for paper production. So in the late 1980s, Japanese companies began to invest heavily in the pulp and paper industry in Alberta and British Columbia.

This investment seemed logical for two reasons. First, Canada was already the largest supplier in the world of pulp and paper to Japan. Second, mills for processing pulp and making paper could be built more cheaply in Canada than in Japan. The government of Alberta was so eager to encourage Japanese investment that it provided a number of financial incentives. These included guaranteed loans to build roads and bridges in tree-harvesting areas. The government also promised to upgrade rail services. For their part, the Japanese companies spent millions of dollars building new mills and millions more leasing vast tracts of forests from the Alberta and B.C. governments.

Criticism of these investments focused on three areas:

▶ The size of the lease holdings. Two of the Japanese companies involved ended up controlling approximately 15% of the province of Alberta.

▶ The secrecy and speed of the negotiations for the land leases. The Japanese companies were granted the timber rights to these lands before any sort of public debate could take place. The people of Alberta were not given the chance to voice their opinion on the leasing of public lands and on the harvesting of the resources on those lands.

▶ In some cases, the leased forests included land claimed by Aboriginal peoples. In one case, this led to a decade-long dispute between the Lubicon Cree of the Peace River region in Alberta and Daishowa Inc. This resulted in a Lubicon Cree-led campaign to boycott Daishowa Inc. paper products.

Supporters of the Japanese companies pointed out that the hundreds of millions of dollars invested in the pulp and paper industry had created jobs for thousands of Canadians as well as paid millions of dollars in taxes to federal and provincial governments.

Figure 16-1 Clear cutting of timber resources occurred extensively on the lands leased to the Japanese pulp and paper companies.

CROSSFIRE

WAS THE DEAL WORTH IT?

Yes

The labour market spin-offs from the Al-Pac pulp mill have been estimated by Mitsubishi and Crestbrook to involve 1300 direct mill-linked jobs (including logging operations) as well as 2600 periphery infrastructure jobs.

—David W. Edgington, *University of British Columbia Geographical Series #49: Japanese Direct Investment in Canada* (Vancouver: UBC Press, 1992), p. 35.

No

Pulp and paper companies came calling from Japan, the United States, and Canada, and within 16 months Alberta had quietly leased public timberlands almost the size of Great Britain to a dozen firms. (Two Japanese-controlled firms got leased rights to tracts covering 15% of the province.) The biggest land rush since the opening of the West ended in December 1988, before most Canadians knew it had begun.

—Andrew Nikiforuk and Ed Struzik, "The Great Forest Sell-Off," *Globe and Mail Report on Business Magazine* (November 1989), p. 57.

Figure 16-2   A Canadian worker at one of the Japanese pulp and paper mills in Alberta.

Japan: An Economic Powerhouse

Japan's importance to Canada can be explained by looking at its position in the global economy. By the 1960s, Japan had become an economic powerhouse. Since its land and economy were in shambles at the end of the World War II, this rapid development has been called an economic miracle. Japan has risen to become the second largest economy in the world after the U.S., and it is the largest creditor nation in the world. This means that more countries owe money to Japan than to any other country.

All this has been accomplished by a country no larger than the state of California with few natural resources other than its 125 million people. Examine the charts and tables on this page and page 53 to develop an idea of the size of Japan's economy.

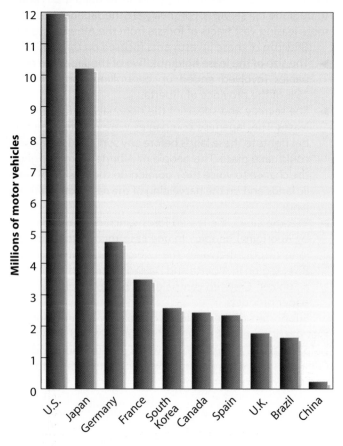

World Motor Vehicle Production, 1997

(Bar graph. Y-axis: Millions of motor vehicles, 0 to 12. X-axis countries: U.S., Japan, Germany, France, South Korea, Canada, Spain, U.K., Brazil, China.)

Figure 16-3   World motor vehicle production. What does this indicate about the scope of manufacturing in Japan?

Source: World Motor Vehicle Data, 1997 Edition.

\multicolumn{4}{c}{**THE WORLD'S 15 LARGEST COMPANIES**}			
Rank	**Company**	**Country**	**Main Product**
1.	General Motors	United States	Motor vehicles
2.	Ford Motor Company	United States	Motor vehicles
3.	Mitsui & Co., Ltd.	Japan	Chemicals, electronics, steel, machinery, banking
4.	Mitsubishi Corporation	Japan	Heavy machinery, home electronics, metals, clothing
5.	Royal Dutch Shell Group	Netherlands	Oil and gas
6.	Itochu Corporation	Japan	Chemicals, electronic machinery, metals
7.	Exxon Corporation	United States	Oil and gas
8.	Wal-Mart Stores, Inc.	United States	Retail merchandising
9.	Marubeni Corporation	Japan	Textiles, metals, chemicals, machinery, wood products
10.	Sumitomo Corporation	Japan	Machinery, electronics, metals, chemicals
11.	Toyota Motor Corporation	Japan	Motor vehicles
12.	General Electric Company	United States	Electrical equipment, appliances
13.	Nissho Iwai Corporation	Japan	Steel, heavy machinery, chemicals
14.	International Business Machines Corporation	United States	Computers, office equipment
15.	Nippon Telegraph & Telephone Corporation	Japan	Telecommunications

Figure 16-4 The world's 15 largest companies in 1997 from *Fortune* magazine's "Global 500 List." Which country has the most companies in the top fifteen?

\multicolumn{2}{c}{**Top Ten Countries by GNP, 1996 (Millions of U.S. dollars)**}	
1. United States	7 433.5
2. Japan	5 149.2
3. Germany	2 364.6
4. France	1 533.6
5. United Kingdom	1 152.1
6. Italy	1 140.5
7. China	906.1
8. Brazil	709.6
9. Canada	569.9
10. Spain	563.2

Source: "Size of the Economy," World Development Indicators CD-ROM, *World Bank*.

Figure 16-5 The top 10 countries by Gross National Product (GNP). GNP measures the total production of a country in a year. It indicates the size of a country's economy. Where does Japan rank? Where you surprised by any countries on the list? Explain.

World Industrial Robot Population, 1991

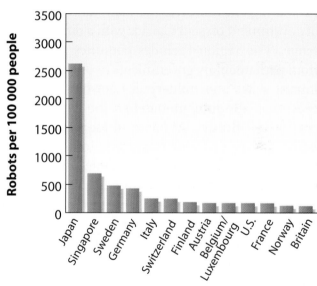

(The total industrial robot population is 5867. Japan's percentage of the total is 44%.)

Figure 16-6 As you can see from this graph, Japan has many more robots working in its factories than any other country in the world. What effect does this have on the cost of producing manufactured goods in Japan? Does it make Japan more or less competitive?

RECONNECT

1. Which sectors of the Canadian economy are of greatest interest to Japanese investors?

2. Re-examine the Crossfire box. Has Japanese investment in Canada been harmful or beneficial to Canada? Support your answer with examples from this chapter.

FOCUS

This section will help you understand
   a. why Canada's self-interest sometimes conflicts with its respect for human rights
   b. why the issue of human rights in China has presented Canada with some difficult decisions to make.

> **Canada uses every appropriate opportunity to speak to the senior leadership regarding China's human rights record, most recently during the Prime Minister's meetings with President Jiang Zemin in November 1997.**
> —A Department of Foreign Affairs and International Trade document, Canada-China Bilateral Relations, April 1998.

Canada's Stand on Human Rights in Asia

Canada is seen around the world as a country that promotes and protects human rights. In the Asia Pacific region, however, the many different forms of government present Canada with a difficult challenge. The region includes countries that range from parliamentary governments to one-party communist states and military dictatorships. There is even one **absolute monarchy**—the tiny, oil-rich country of Brunei. Many of these governments place limits on individual freedoms, that in Canada, we would find unacceptable. Under some of the more repressive governments, people who participate in political protests may be imprisoned, sent into exile, or even executed.

Whenever a trading partner abuses the human rights of its citizens, Canada must decide how to react. Its choices fall into three categories:

▶ to ignore the abuses and continue to reap the benefits of trade with the country.

▶ to sever its trade ties with the country until the abuses stop.

▶ to continue to trade with the country but work through diplomatic channels to improve the country's record on human rights.

It is this last approach that Canada has taken in its dealings with China.

Canada's Relations with China

Canada's relationship with the People's Republic of China is a good illustration of the human rights chal-

lenge Canada faces in dealing with some countries in Asia Pacific. In 1996, China became Canada's fifth-largest trading partner. This economic relationship grew even stronger the following year when Hong Kong, Canada's tenth-largest trading partner at the time, was returned to China by Great Britain.

China has been a one-party state since 1949 when Mao Zedong's communists assumed control. Many human rights taken for granted in Canada, such as freedom of speech, freedom of the press and freedom of religion, cannot be exercised by Chinese citizens.

Canada is faced with a dilemma in China: how to convince the Chinese government to grant its

Figure 17-1 A man stands in front of a tank on the Avenue of Eternal Peace on June 5, 1989, a day after the Tiananmen Square massacre. Why were the protesters occupying Tiananmen Square? Was the protest successful? Explain your answer.

citizens basic human rights while still maintaining its profitable trade deals with China. This dilemma has been aggravated in recent years by the Tiananmen Square massacre and political repression in Tibet.

Tiananmen Square

In April 1989, Chinese students occupied the huge Tiananmen Square in the heart of Beijing, China's capital city. They were protesting against the lack of human rights in China. This occupation of Tiananmen Square was especially embarrassing to the Chinese government because the square had become a well recognized symbol of the People's Republic of China. It is in this square that foreign dignitaries are greeted on their visits to China and that many national celebrations are held.

After two months of continuing demonstrations, soldiers of the People's Liberation Army used tanks and other heavy arms to sweep the protesters out of the square. According to some reports, more than 1000 students died in this bloody clash. Others were imprisoned, and in July the government began public executions of student leaders.

The Chinese students who died in Tiananmen Square were asking for the same democratic freedoms that are guaranteed to everyone in Canada. The first reaction of the Canadian government was

Figure 17-2 A rally in Hong Kong on the ninth anniversary of the Tiananmen Square massacre. Many people had feared that political demonstrations like this would be banned once Hong Kong returned to China. But this rally, held almost a year after the hand over, attracted 40 000 people and was peaceful throughout.

to condemn the massacre and cancel some minor trade agreements. After little more than a year, however, diplomatic relations were back to normal. Although many of the student protesters were still held in Chinese prisons, Canadian business people continued investing in China's booming economy. In 1994, Prime Minister Jean Chrétien organized a trip to China by a large group of Canadian business people and political leaders. The sole purpose of

CROSSFIRE

IS CANADA'S APPROACH TO

HUMAN RIGHTS IN CHINA MORALLY CORRECT?

They (foreigners) cannot understand that if social turmoil erupts, then the production and the life of the people would be greatly affected, especially in China… In other words, during the 1989…political incident (Tiananmen Square massacre), had the then Chinese government failed to adopt resolute measures, then we could not have enjoyed today's stability, and without stability, the 1.2 billion Chinese people could not possibly enjoy this good situation brought about by reform and opening up that we are enjoying today.

—Jiang Zemin, President of the People's Republic of China, quoted in *The Globe and Mail* (December 1, 1997), p. A12.

Our relationship with China cannot, and must not, be defined as a stand-off between trade and human rights. We are determined to advance in both of these areas, indeed, in many areas.

—Lloyd Axworthy, Minister of Foreign Affairs, in a speech at the University of Toronto, March 24, 1997.

The western democracies—including Canada—are averting their eyes from the bloodstains on Tiananmen Square as they compete for China's immense markets. By not calling China's rulers to account for their continuing lawless behaviour, we could be making an immense strategic mistake. We could be laying out a future in which a neo-imperial Chinese superpower, run by cold-blooded tyrants, will be the economic bully of the 21st century.

—Matt Hughes, Canadian novelist, quoted in *The Vancouver Sun* (March 27, 1997), p. E2.

the trip was to drum up business for Canada in China. Canadian exports to China jumped by nearly 50% after the Team Canada visit, totalling $3.4 billion in 1995. In 1996, Canada approved a $51-million sale of military arms to China.

Tibet

The violation of human rights in the Chinese-controlled region of Tibet has also become a public issue. For Canada, it once again places the benefits of trade against a backdrop of international condemnation of human rights abuses committed by the People's Republic of China.

For most of the 20th century, Tibet has been one of the most isolated regions in the world. The Tibetan people have a language, culture, and religion which is distinct from the main population group in China known as the Han Chinese. They developed a unique culture based on a deep religious belief in Buddhism. Tibetans look at their spiritual leader, the Dalai Lama, as not only a divine presence, but also as a government leader.

In 1950, China invaded eastern Tibet. The Chinese army quickly defeated the poorly equipped Tibetan army, and in 1951 the government of the Dalai Lama was forced to sign an agreement recognizing Tibet as part of China.

The occupation of Tibet by the Chinese army and government officials, along with the lack of respect which Tibetans felt the Chinese showed to their traditions and culture, led to a violent uprising in 1959. The rebellion resulted in a brutal crackdown by Chinese authorities. The Dalai Lama, along with 100 000 Tibetans, fled to neighbouring India where a government-in-exile was set up.

The decade known as the Cultural Revolution in China would be an even more tumultuous period for Tibetans. From 1966 to 1976, nearly 4000 Buddhist monasteries, along with religious statues and works of art, were destroyed. Thousands of Buddhist monks were forcefully removed from temples and monasteries by mobs of Chinese known as the Red Guards who embraced the idea that all religious beliefs should be destroyed.

Civil unrest continued into the 1980s and 1990s. Between 1987 and 1989 several anti-Chinese riots occurred in the capital city of Lhasa. Severe repression was used to put down the revolts and in 1989 **martial law** was declared. In 1995, the death of the

Figure 17-3 What is the point of view of the cartoonist? Do you agree? Support your opinion.

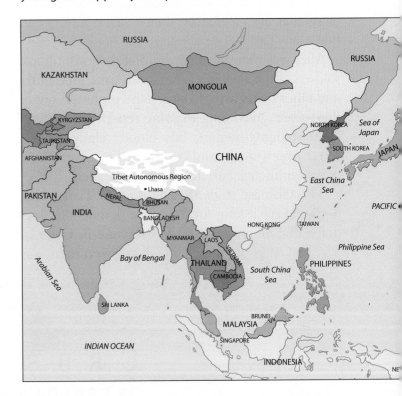

Figure 17-4 Tibet is officially called the Tibet Autonomous Region and occupies a huge plateau (1 228 000 square kilometres) in southwest China marked by the highest mountains in the world including Mount Everest. Even Lhasa—the capital and largest city—has an elevation of 3600 metres. For this reason Tibet is known as "the roof of the world." Based on the above map, why does the People's Republic of China view Tibet as strategically important?

Panchen Lama, who is the second highest religious figure in Tibet, resulted in a religious and political dispute. The Dalai Lama, still living in exile in India, chose a Tibetan boy **reincarnation** of the Panchen Lama with the help of several high ranking Buddhist monks. Over the objections of the Dalai Lama, the Chinese government selected another boy to become the next Panchen Lama. The child selected by the Dalai Lama was put under house arrest in Tibet.

The Chinese government has taken some positive steps in Tibet. During the 1990s, schools, hospitals, and roads were built and some religious buildings have been restored. Economic development has also been given priority. This resulted in a large influx of Han Chinese looking for jobs that were unavailable in other parts of China. In 1950, nearly 100% of the population was Tibetan, but by the late 1990s up to 20% of Tibet's inhabitants were Han Chinese. Exiled Tibetans charge that this is a deliberate attempt by the People's Republic of China to overwhelm the Tibetan people with a loyal Chinese population.

Canada and Tibet

In 1989, as a result of the Tiananmen Square massacre, Canada and other countries sponsored a United Nations resolution condemning the abuse of human rights in China. This yearly resolution was also seen as international disapproval of Chinese policies in Tibet. In 1997, for the first time Canada, along with other important European countries, decided to withdraw its support of this resolution. The Canadian government opted to use quiet diplomacy in attempting to improve China's human-rights record.

BIOGRAPHY

Subject: Dalai Lama

Dates: Born, July 6, 1935

Most Notable Accomplishment: Won the Nobel Peace Prize in 1989 for his non-violent attempts to resist Chinese control of Tibet.

Thumbnail Sketch: The Dalai Lama was born Llamo Dhondrub in a small village called Takster in northwestern Tibet. At the age of two, in accordance with Tibetan tradition, he was recognized as the reincarnation of his predecessor the 13th Dalai Lama.

On November 17, 1950 the Dalai Lama assumed full political power after about 80 000 People's Liberation Army soldiers invaded Tibet. In 1954, he went to China to talk peace with Mao Zedong and other Chinese leaders. Over the next five years he continued to seek a peaceful solution to the Sino-Tibetan conflict, but China's repressive policies led to an uprising in 1959. The rebellion was brutally crushed by the Chinese army and the Dalai Lama was forced to leave Tibet with about 100 000 Tibetans. He was 24 years old at the time. The Dalai Lama set up a government-in-exile in India, and since then has led the effort to re-establish a Tibetan form of government and to preserve Tibetan culture and heritage.

Significant Quote: "The path of non-violence must remain a matter of principle in our long and difficult quest for freedom. It is my firm belief that this approach is the most beneficial and practical course in the long run… Through our non-violent freedom struggle we are also setting an example and thus contributing to the promotion of a global political culture of non-violence and dialogue."

—*Dalai Lama in a statement on the 39th anniversary of the Tibetan National Uprising Day, March 10, 1998.*

Figure 17-5   The Dalai Lama accepting the Nobel Peace prize in 1989.

RECONNECT

1. What is the dilemma Canada faces with China? Explain fully.

2. Assume you are the prime minister of Canada. Write a brief speech indicating your position on the issue of human rights in China.

FOCUS

This section will help you understand
   a. the system of government in Indonesia
   b. the dilemma that human rights violations in Indonesia pose for Canadian foreign policy.

Indonesia: Economic Development vs. Human Rights

Indonesia presents Canada with another troublesome challenge in international relations. The government of Indonesia stresses political stability and economic development at the expense of human rights. Between 1967 and 1998, the president of Indonesia was a retired army general named Suharto. Many of Suharto's cabinet members were also from the military. Although general elections were held every five years, Suharto severely restricted all forms of political opposition and any criticism by the press. Suharto himself appointed the leaders of the two opposition parties.

On the positive side, the stable government Indonesia enjoyed for 30 years made it possible for the country to realize significant economic gains. Foreign investment from Western countries such as Canada and the U.S. increased over this period, but especially in the 1990s. For example, in 1998, Canada had direct investments in Indonesia worth $6.6 billion. Overall the standard of living and education level of the population has increased.

On the negative side, there is still widespread poverty in Indonesia and a great deal of corruption among government officials. Even worse, human rights violations, often organized by the Indonesian army, have been directed against political opponents as well as ethnic minorities like the Chinese.

MAP STUDY — INDONESIA

Indonesia is a Southeast Asian country with the fourth-largest population in the world. It covers more than 13 000 islands, 6000 of which are inhabited. More than 195 million people live in Indonesia, about half of them on the island of Java. The vast majority of Indonesians practise Islam, making it the largest Muslim country in the world. Although it is rich in primary resources, Indonesia has a low standard of living compared with Canada. What might be some of the difficulties in governing a country like Indonesia?

BIOGRAPHY

Subject: Suharto

Dates: Born, 1921

Most Notable Accomplishment: President of Indonesia from 1967 to 1998.

Thumbnail Sketch: Suharto has had a greater impact on present-day Indonesia than any other leader. He was an officer in the Indonesian guerrilla army when the country gained its independence from the Netherlands in 1949. After a period of political and economic turmoil in the early 1960s, Suharto led the army in 1965 in crushing a coup by the Indonesian Communist Party. He banned the Communist Party and broke off relations with the People's Republic of China, while establishing closer relations with the U.S. Over the next several months, nearly one million Indonesians were killed throughout Indonesia. Much of the violence was directed against Communist Party members and the small Chinese minority.

Figure 18-1 President Suharto with family members.

In 1967, General Suharto officially became president of Indonesia and enjoyed almost absolute power over the next 31 years. He appointed many other army officers to positions of power in the government and clamped down on all forms of dissent.

Indonesia's economy improved under Suharto, but at the same time there was a great deal of corruption. Members of Suharto's family became incredibly wealthy. Foreign companies found it was easier to do business in Indonesia if they made one of Suharto's children a business partner.

In 1997, Indonesia was hit hard by the economic downturn in Asia Pacific. The collapsing economy and violent riots throughout Indonesia finally forced Suharto to resign in May 1998.

Figure 18-2 Indonesia's collapsing economy and widespread discontent over Suharto's repressive government led to riots in the capital of Jakarta and other cities throughout Indonesia. Some reports indicated that up to 1000 people were killed. Much of the terror was directed against the small but economically powerful, Chinese community.

Primary Source
"MY BROTHER DIED THERE"

As a 21-year-old Canadian university student, I hardly have a professional interest in what is going on in far-off East Timor, but I certainly have a personal one—last fall, my brother died there. Kamal was 20 and on his way home to Malaysia during a break from his university studies in Australia.

Then, on November 12, Indonesian troops opened fire on a Timorese crowd mourning the death of an independence sympathizer. Exactly how many died is the subject of great debate, but my brother was among them. His body was found half a kilometre from the site of the massacre. How it got there has yet to be explained.

—Li-lien Gibbons, *The Globe and Mail* (February 10, 1992), p. A15.

CaseStudy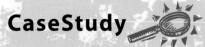

THE INVASION AND OCCUPATION OF EAST TIMOR

Timor is a large island to the east of Indonesia's main island of Java. When Indonesia gained independence from the Netherlands in 1949, it controlled the western half of Timor, while the eastern half remained under the control of Portugal. In 1975, nine days after East Timor declared its independence from Portugal, Indonesian troops invaded. A year later Indonesia claimed East Timor as its 27th province. The annexation was never recognized by the UN, which continued to regard Portugal as the administering power.

During the invasion and occupation, about 200 000 East Timorese died from war, famine, disease, and executions. Since the total population of East Timor was only about 650 000, this means that over 30% of the people died as a result of the invasion and the forced relocation that followed. The United Nations passed several resolutions demanding that Indonesia withdraw and allow elections to determine what the people of East Timor wanted. Indonesia ignored the UN.

The East Timorese remained resentful about the invasion, and many have never accepted Indonesian rule. The Indonesian army punished any public expression in favour of independence. Occasionally violence broke out. In 1991, the army fired upon a peaceful demonstration in the city of Dili, killing about 200 marchers. In 1996, two East Timorese were awarded the Nobel Peace Prize. This was an international embarrassment for Indonesia.

The fall of Suharto in May 1998 gave many Timorese new hope. Three weeks after coming to power, Indonesia's new leader President B.J. Habibie, suggested giving limited special status to East Timor. In August, Portugal and Indonesia agreed to begin talks on limited self-government of East Timor. In January 1999, Indonesia offered East Timor special autonomy with control over its own internal affairs.

Although many countries have condemned Indonesia for its actions in East Timor, most of them, like Canada, have at the same time sought stronger economic links. Human rights groups around the world have criticized Indonesia's trading partners for not taking a stronger stand in regard to East Timor.

Figure 18-3   Jose Ramos Horta and Bishop Carlos Filipe Ximenes Belo of East Timor were awarded the Nobel Peace Prize in 1996. Both men have criticized the Indonesian occupation of East Timor. Bishop Belo has survived two assassination attempts. Horta, a leader of the independence struggle, has lived in exile for more than 20 years. Why was the government of Indonesia offended by the international recognition given to Belo and Horta?

Canadian Trade and Aid with Indonesia

As one of Asia's fastest-growing and largest economies, Indonesia has been an important trading partner for Canada. In 1995, Indonesia was Canada's eighteenth-largest export market and the largest in Southeast Asia. Major Canadian exports to Indonesia are grain, pulp and paper, machinery, and organic chemicals, while Canada imports textiles, shoes, and rubber products. In addition, Canada has large Indonesian investments in mining and oil and gas.

Canada also provides development assistance to improve living conditions in Indonesia. This aid was halted after the massacre in East Timor in 1991, but relations have since returned to normal. In 1995, Canada's aid to Indonesia exceeded $31 million. In 1996, a high-profile Team Canada visit took place to seek more business deals.

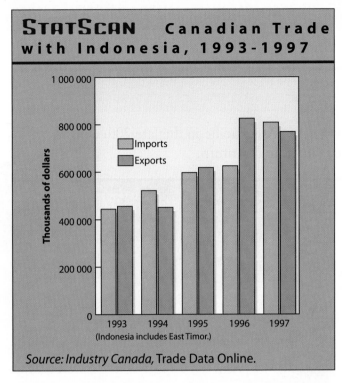

StatScan Canadian Trade with Indonesia, 1993-1997

Thousands of dollars

- Imports
- Exports

(Indonesia includes East Timor.)

Source: Industry Canada, Trade Data Online.

Figure 18-5   Canadian trade with Indonesia, 1993-1997. Which country benefits most according to the graph? Explain. Look at the years 1996 and 1997. What effect did the economic downturn and political turmoil have on Canadian-Indonesian trade? Canadian exports to Indonesia declined dramatically to 500 million in 1998.

Figure 18-6 Despite Indonesia's booming economy in the early 1990s, many of its people continue to live in poverty. It is these sorts of conditions that Canada's development aid to Indonesia is designed to improve.

CROSSFIRE

SHOULD CANADA DO BUSINESS WITH INDONESIA?

Yes

The Canada-Indonesia Business Council has said that reforms to foreign investment rules implemented last year by the Indonesian government have made it more attractive for Canadian firms to do business in the world's sixth-fastest growing economy. Indonesia is Canada's largest export market in Southeast Asia, with bilateral trade exceeding $1 billion annually.

—From "Indonesia welcomes B.C. power expertise," *The Vancouver Sun* (June 27, 1995), p. A10.

No

The signal the government (Canadian) is sending is that they will send weapons to any country, no matter what their human rights record is, no matter how many people they are killing.

—David Webster, member of the East Timor Alert Network, quoted in *The Vancouver Sun* (September 27, 1996), p. A2.

I have enormous respect for Canada. Its grants for rural development in East Timor are greatly appreciated. But Canada and the U.S. must call for a referendum in East Timor on self-determination, under UN supervision.

—Jose Ramos Horta, Nobel Peace Prize winner from East Timor. Quoted on a visit to Vancouver in *The Vancouver Sun* (March 8, 1997).

RECONNECT

1. Describe the human rights problems facing Indonesia.

2. In your opinion what kind of relations should Canada have with Indonesia? Write a paragraph to defend your answer.

FOCUS

This section will help you understand
a. the background to the economic downturn in Asia Pacific in the late 20th century
b. how Canada has been affected by the economic downturn.

Overview of an Economic Crisis

As the end of the century approached, experts spoke of a new global economy which would soon revolve around the dynamic Asia Pacific region. This outlook changed drastically in 1997 once Asia Pacific found itself in the middle of a severe economic downturn. The first country to be affected was Thailand. The value of its currency—the baht—declined sharply in relation to the U.S. dollar on July 2, 1997. This **devaluation** of the baht put severe pressure on Thai banks and finance companies which had borrowed large sums of U.S. dollars. Because of the devalued Thai baht, the cost of repaying these loans rose so high that many companies were forced into bankruptcy. At the same time the value of real estate, much of it purchased with borrowed money, dropped sharply. Soon thousands of Thai workers found themselves unemployed.

This pattern repeated itself in Malaysia and then Indonesia, where massive political and social unrest exploded, and quickly spread to other countries in Asia Pacific. In South Korea, which had become a global economic power, a near meltdown of its currency occurred.

The Asian Flu

Commentators referred to this economic downturn as the **Asian flu** because it spread like a contagious virus. The characteristics of the Asian flu were:
► a sharp decline in the value of currencies in relation to the U.S. dollar. Most Asia Pacific countries experienced severe loss in the value of their currencies.
► widespread bankruptcies of banks which had loaned out huge amounts for questionable investments, especially in real estate.
► increased unemployment as workers were laid off, either by bankrupt companies or those cutting back on production.

Figure 19-1 The financial crisis in Indonesia was so severe that in July 1998 more than 100 000 people gathered to pray for relief from the country's economic woes.

► **inflation**, especially in the prices of imported goods. This tended to raise the prices of essential goods like fuel and food which caused widespread hardship.
► a decline in foreign investment as investors looked for safer places than Asia to invest.
► record-breaking drops in the value of company shares traded on local stock exchanges.
► an overall economic slowdown as people purchased only the most essential goods.

Economists say that an economy which shrinks, rather than grows, for half a year, is suffering a recession. Because of the Asian flu, most Asia Pacific countries are now in the grips of a recession. This means that the standard of living for people in Asia Pacific will decrease. The poor will be especially hard hit. The question for many is whether or not the economic downturn will extend beyond Asia Pacific to become a global recession or even a depression.

NewsFlash

The bursting of Asia's bubble
by Raju Gopalakrishnan

JAKARTA—The human tragedies spawned by Asia's raging financial crisis have only just begun, analysts and economists say. For months to come, millions more will be thrown out of work and countless families will lack money for food.

"In the next 12 months, I see things getting worse in terms of social instability and people's livelihood," said Sandra Lawson, political strategist at Goldman Sachs in Hong Kong.

"Unemployment is going to continue…and I'm concerned about social unrest in all of the four crisis countries. These, said Lawson, are Indonesia, Malaysia, South Korea, and Thailand—all nations where until last year a willingness to work was usually the only requirement for a reasonably comfortable and sometimes prosperous life.

The relentless flight of Western capital since a regional currency crisis started just over 12 months ago has dealt a body blow to these economies and made a mockery of their standards of living.

In Indonesia, almost half the country's 200 million people will be unable to afford food by the end of 1998, the government says.

Unemployment has doubled in Thailand in 12 months. It has almost tripled in South Korea and Malaysia.

Seoul's national statistics office says about 7000 people are losing jobs each day. Eighty per cent of workers have taken pay cuts since the crisis started last year, the local chamber of commerce says.

In Indonesia, some analysts have estimated the contraction in the economy at 25 per cent this year, about the most severe that any nation has gone through since World War II.

Huge resources have gone into trying to ease the crisis in Asia. The International Monetary Fund has drawn up $120 billion rescue plans for the battered economies of Indonesia, Thailand, and South Korea.

The IMF has laid great stress on structural reform, especially in the banking sector, but these efforts will take time. Meanwhile, currencies are depreciating, more people are out of jobs, and poverty is increasing.

Governments have changed in all three nations that received IMF succour, but the changes they in turn must bring in are overwhelming.

Source: *The Toronto Star* (July 6, 1998), p. A10.

Figure 19-2 Striking workers at Hyundai Motor Co., South Korea's largest auto maker. Workers occupied Hyundai factories and several union leaders were arrested. Other industrial workers involved in work stoppages pushed the total number of workers on strike to well over 50 000. Many Korean workers considered lifetime employment to be a right, but new laws made it easier for companies to lay them off. How would investors and workers look at this type of law differently? Explain.

Figure 19-3 Koreans contributed jewellery to the governments as a way of helping it overcome balance of payments problems. What does this show about the feeling of many Koreans towards their country?

The International Monetary Fund

The International Monetary Fund (IMF) is an agency of the UN. Its main purpose is to stabilize exchange rates and make loans to countries experiencing financial problems. The IMF came under criticism during the economic downturn in Asia Pacific. Criticism came from two sources: donor countries and receiving countries.

Donor countries believed:

▶ the IMF loaned out too much money without sufficient guarantees of being repaid.

▶ the IMF did not analyse the conditions in Asia Pacific closely enough to prevent the economic crisis.

▶ in spite of huge loans, the economic crisis worsened rather than stabilized.

Receiving countries believed:

▶ loans by the IMF were too small to help countries re-establish their collapsed economies.

▶ the IMF conditions caused hardships for ordinary citizens. This, in turn, created political and social unrest. For example, countries have been required to close banks with credit problems, raise taxes to decrease government deficits, and end subsidies to fuel and essential foods like rice. (See chapter 25 for more information on the IMF.)

CaseStudy

THE ASIAN FLU AND CANADA

Globalization means that events often have an impact around the world. This has been the case with the Asian flu. Economic troubles in one Asia Pacific country have spread to the entire region. Soon Canada's economy also began to suffer. There have been many examples in previous chapters of the benefits of interdependence. But the economic downturn in Asia Pacific shows the harm that global interdependence can inflict on the livelihood of a country like Canada.

British Columbia was the first province in Canada to feel the impact since a larger share of its economy is economically dependent on Asia Pacific. During the late 1980s and early 1990s, B.C. had benefited greatly from links to Asia Pacific, and especially to Japan, since its products were in great demand. B.C. also benefited from the large number of business immigrants from Asia Pacific who spent money setting up businesses and buying real estate. Because of this, B.C.'s economy outperformed the rest of Canada.

But the Asian flu reduced demand in Asia Pacific for all products, especially imports. With devalued currencies, these countries could no longer afford to purchase as much as before. To make matters worse, the lion's share of B.C.'s (and Canada's) exports to Asia Pacific consisted of commodities. A commodity is an economic term for bulk goods which are traded between countries. It is different from manufactured goods which require more labour and technology. Examples of commodities are metals, livestock, oil and gas, grain, and lumber. Because demand for commodities in Asia Pacific slumped, worldwide prices fell. Examine the following charts to determine why Canada, and especially B.C., would be harmed by the Asian flu.

Top Ten Canadian Exports to Japan, 1994	
Goods	**Amount (millions of $Canadian)**
lumber logs and plywood	$2 216 000
coal	$1 205 000
wood pulp	$658 000
fish and seafood	$638 000
canola	$476 000
copper	$357 000
chemicals	$290 000
wheat	$287 000
aluminum	$272 000
paper	$267 000

Top Ten Canadian Imports from Japan, 1994	
Goods	**Amount (millions of $Canadian)**
passenger cars	$2 264 000
auto parts	$1 464 000
telecommunications equipment	$1 227 000
computers	$1 192 000
general machinery	$1 010 000
commercial vehicles	$339 000
precision instruments	$280 000
games and toys	$234 000
transportation equipment (excluding cars)	$231 000
televisions, radios, phonographs	$216 000

Figure 19-4 What is the difference between Canadian imports from Japan and Canadian exports? Why would Canada suffer from a lower worldwide demand for commodities?

CaseStudy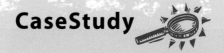

THE CANADIAN DOLLAR AND THE ASIAN FLU

Most experts believe an economy as dependent on commodity exports as Canada's will be especially hard hit by the Asian flu. A direct result of the Asian flu, they say, has been the declining value of the Canadian dollar. Other experts also blame Canada's taxation rates as well as government debt.

The value of the Canadian dollar, like most currencies, is measured against the U.S. dollar which has been the world standard since the end of World War II. The actual value of a currency is worked out by a complex process which involves multinational corporations and banks, as well as governments. Since governments frequently need large amounts of foreign currencies to conduct business, money traders buy and sell billions of dollars worth of different currencies daily around the world on their behalf.

Due to the speed of high-tech communications, an event in Thailand can influence traders in Chicago to buy or sell immediately. Ultimately, a currency's value shows how much it is desired by money traders. This, in turn, usually reflects how well a country's economy is doing. Currency exchange rates, whether high or low, can have an impact on a country's economy and the standard of living of its citizens.

Sometimes governments even buy up their own currency. They usually do this in order to maintain its value. To do this a government must usually pay in a stable currency like the U.S. dollar. Since billions of dollars are traded daily, this can strain the resources of even large countries. At the beginning of the economic crisis, several Asia Pacific countries, such as Thailand and South Korea, attempted to prop up their currencies by buying them with U.S. dollars but soon gave up. This resulted in an even deeper devaluation of the currencies.

StatScan   The Impact of Exchange Rates

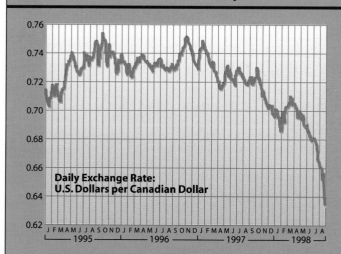

Daily Exchange Rate: U.S. Dollars per Canadian Dollar

Figure 19-5 What is highest value of the Canadian dollar? What is the lowest? Since the Asian flu first broke out in Thailand in July 1997, what has happened to the value of the Canadian dollar? How did this affect trade and tourism between the U.S. and Canada?

EXCHANGE RATES

High exchange rate
- imports increase because goods from foreign countries are cheaper.
- exports decrease because they are more costly to foreign countries.
- foreign investment is encouraged since property in foreign countries is cheaper to buy.
- travel abroad is cheaper.

Low exchange rate
- imports decrease because goods from foreign countries are more expensive
- exports increase because they are cheaper for foreign countries to buy.
- investment by foreigners is encouraged because their money goes a long way.
- tourism is encouraged since foreign currencies can buy more.

RECONNECT

1. Explain why the economic downturn in Asia Pacific is referred to as the Asian flu?

2. Write a paragraph describing the effects of the Asian flu on Canada.

20 European Immigration up to World War I

FOCUS

This section will help you understand
   a. the impact of European immigration on Canada up to World War I
   b. the early 20th century was the first time in Canada's history that immigrants from European countries other than Britain and France arrived in significant numbers.

TIMELINE 1900-2000

1905 — Clifford Sifton resigns after 10 years of being responsible for immigration as minister of the interior.

1911 — Sir Wilfrid Laurier and his Liberal Party are defeated over the issue of reciprocity with the U.S.

1913 — Immigration to Canada reaches a peak of 400 870.

1914-18 — Canada makes a major contribution to the British war effort in World War I.

1921 — William Lyon Mackenzie King and his Liberal Party are elected.

1922 — Prime Minister King refuses a British request to send Canadian soldiers to fight on behalf of the British Empire during the Chanak Affair.

1923 — Canada negotiates the Halibut Treaty directly with the United States rather than through the British Foreign Office.

1926 — Prime Minister King wins the election after the King-Byng Crisis by claiming that the Canadian Parliament has supremacy over a British-appointed governor general.

1931 — Canada achieves autonomy when the Statute of Westminster recognizes Canada's control (without British interference) over its own foreign affairs.

1939-45 — Canada supports Britain during World War II.

1945 — The United Nations is established in San Francisco.
The World Bank and International Monetary Fund are established.

1956 — Prime Minister Lester Pearson proposes the first UN peacekeeping mission after the Suez Crisis in the Middle East.

1958 — The Treaty of Rome establishes a "common market" which becomes the groundwork for a future unified Europe.

1965 — The European Community is set up to link western European governments and economies.

1970 — The international organization of French-speaking countries, known as la Francophonie, is established. Canada is a founding member.

1971 — The Commonwealth of Nations declares the equality of all member countries.

1991 — Communist Soviet Union collapses and the Cold War ends.

1992 — The European Union (EU) adopts a single parliament.

1995 — Tension arises between Canada and the EU during "the Turbot War."

1996 — The U.S. passes the Helms-Burton Act which punishes countries like Canada for continuing to trade with Cuba.

1999 — EU countries begin to use a single currency known as the Euro in bank transactions.

Canada's Population at the End of the 19th Century

One of the most important links between Canada and Europe is immigration. The movement of European peoples into the land that was to become Canada began in the 17th century when settlers from France arrived in the area around the St. Lawrence River. After the British victory in the Seven Years War (1756-63), French immigration stopped and British merchants and settlers began to arrive in what was called British North America.

Canada's population would be dominated by these two immigrant groups for the next 150 years. By 1901 Canada's relatively small population of 5 371 315 was 57% of British origin and 31% of French origin. The waves of immigrants that arrived in the early years of the 20th century would have two major impacts on Canada's population:

▶ the overall size of the population would post a dramatic 25% increase in the 10-year period between 1901 and 1911, and

▶ there would be a gradual shift in the pattern of immigrantion. Many people came from countries such as Russia, Poland, the Ukraine and Germany, which were not traditional sources for Canadian immigrants. The process of changing Canada into a racially diverse and multicultural country had just begun.

The Laurier Years

Sir Wilfrid Laurier was elected prime minister in 1896 and held office until he was defeated in the election of 1911. During the Laurier years, such large numbers of immigrants poured into the Prairies that in 1905 two new provinces, Saskatchewan and Alberta, were carved out of the Northwest Territories.

At the same time, Canadian cities experienced impressive growth. This growth in immigration continued up to the beginning of World War I in 1914. In spite of increasing numbers of immigrants from outside Britain, the connection to Britain remained strong with the non-French part of Canada's population still mostly of British origin. Also, many of the European immigrants from outside Britain adopted aspects of the English-speaking culture. One of the most important adopted cultural traits was the English language itself.

Figure 20-1 Sir Wilfrid Laurier was prime minister for 15 years during a time of economic prosperity. What effect did the worldwide economic boom have on Canada's drive to settle the Prairies?

Figure 20-2 This poster was produced by the Canadian Department of the Interior. What are the different appeals to immigrants displayed on this poster? To which groups of potential immigrants was it directed?

EyeWitness

"Land to the European was sacred"

It was so often letters. What people today call word-of-mouth. Frau Schmidt in Upper Silesia would be boasting that her Herman had 320 acres of wheat land in Saskatchewan and the word would get around. Big stuff. That dumb cluck. Left four years ago with nothing but his clothes and a packsack, and now he's got 320 acres of land. You know what I mean. Land to the European was sacred. That's what nine out of 10 of their wars was about. Canada there, all that land. My God!

So if it was Germany or Russia or England you came from, you'd send letters to your home town and the letters would get passed around. Talked about. Soon another family would pack up, sell what they couldn't carry, and be off to Canada.

—Second-generation German farmer in Saskatchewan quoted in Barry Broadfoot, *The Pioneer Years, 1895-1914* (Toronto: Doubleday, 1976), p. 23.

CaseStudy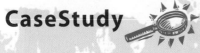

WHY DID IMMIGRANTS COME TO CANADA? PUSH-PULL FACTORS

Pull Factors

During Laurier's time as prime minister there were many factors that "pulled" immigrants into Canada.

• The most important pull factor was the worldwide economic boom. The boom created a strong demand for products that were Canadian specialties, such as natural resources and farm produce, especially wheat. As the demand for wheat went up, so did its price. Higher prices meant that immigrant farmers on the Prairies had a better chance of making a profit.

• A new wheat hybrid, Marquis, ripened about two weeks earlier than other types. This made the likelihood of harvesting the crop much greater on the Prairies, where winter could arrive quite early.

• Technological advances, such as the improved seed driller and the threshing machine, made it possible to farm larger tracts of land. Other pull factors were the result of government action.

• The **Crowsnest Pass Agreement** lowered transportation costs for Prairie farmers shipping their grain to Fort William (Thunder Bay) on Lake Superior.

• The government stopped giving large land grants to railways and pressured other landholders to put their land up for sale to immigrant farmers.

• Even more importantly, the government offered immigrants 160 acres (65 hectares) with an option to buy another 160 acres at a low price, on the condition that they farm the land for three years.

• The Minister of the Interior Clifford Sifton also organized an effective advertising campaign in Europe to lure immigrants to Canada.

All of these changes made the Prairies a more desirable destination for immigrants.

Figure 20-3   Charles Saunders, the hybridist who created the Marquis strain of wheat, examines a field of the new wheat. Marquis avoided the frost damage other strains were vulnerable to by ripening up to two weeks earlier. When ground, it produced a very high-grade flour. Available for commercial production by 1907, Marquis was one of the factors that lured immigrant farmers to the Canadian Prairies.

Push Factors

Immigrants from Europe also had good reasons for wanting to leave their homelands. These included:

• The threat of war. The sprawling empires of Russia and Austria-Hungary were hotbeds of protest and outright rebellion. For example, in Russia the 1905 Revolution almost succeeded in overthrowing its monarchy.

• Religious persecution. For instance, in 1899, 7427 **Doukhobors** settled in the future province of Saskatchewan, where they were given 300 000 free hectares of farmland. The Doukhobors were fleeing religious persecution in Russia. The Jews were another group which often faced persecution. In Russia at the turn of the century Jewish settlements faced violent **pogroms** which were frequently aided and even organized by units in the Russian imperial army. By 1911, over 76 000 Jews were living in Canada.

• The rise of nationalism by dominant population groups in Russia and Austria- Hungary often led to the ill treatment of minority groups. Germans and Ukrainians in Russia and Croats and Slovaks in Austria-Hungary were examples of this kind of discrimination.

• Population growth because of the Industrial Revolution. As a result, most of Europe, in contrast to Canada, was densely populated and land was scarce. In one extreme case in Austria-Hungary, the province of Galicia had over 1 million farms smaller than eight acres.

Figure 20-4   Doukhobor immigrants in Saskatchewan in 1902. Why did they leave their homelands to settle in a country they knew so little about?

• Large numbers of people living in rural areas in Europe, including Britain, did not benefit from the worldwide economic boom. This was because much of the land was controlled by wealthy landowners who used poor peasants as cheap labour. The thousands of slum children shipped to Canada alone from Britain were another sad example of economic hardship during this time.

In most cases a combination of push and pull factors led immigrants to seek a better life in Canada.

BIOGRAPHY

Subject: Sir Clifford Sifton

Dates: **1861-1929**

Most Notable Accomplishment: As minister of the Interior from 1896 to 1905, Sifton successfully organized a government program that brought hundreds of thousands of immigrants to the Canadian West.

Thumbnail Sketch: Sifton was born in what is now Ontario but moved to Manitoba when he was 14 years old. After graduating from Victoria College in Toronto, he became a lawyer in 1882 in Manitoba. He was elected as a Liberal MLA in Brandon, Manitoba in 1888 and three years later became the attorney general in the provincial cabinet. When Laurier swept to power in 1896, he appointed Sifton minister of the interior. Sifton was soon recognized as the most influential member of Parliament from the West. He negotiated the Crowsnest Pass Agreement with the Canadian Pacific Railway, and in 1903 argued the Canadian side in the Alaska Boundary Dispute. An energetic and capable minister, Sifton designed a program to attract immigrant farmers to the Canadian Prairies. His program featured a massive advertising campaign and paid agents in Britain, Europe, and the U.S. Sifton was criticized for wooing immigrants from eastern and central Europe. After a falling out with Laurier in 1905, Sifton quit his cabinet post. In the election of 1911, he actively campaigned against Laurier on the issue of reciprocity.

Figure 20-5   Sir Clifford Sifton.

Significant Quote: "When I speak of quality I have in mind, I think, something that is quite different from what is in the mind of the average writer or speaker upon the question of immigration. I think a stalwart peasant in a sheep-skin coat, born on the soil, whose forefathers have been farmers for ten generations, with a stout wife and a half-dozen children, is good quality."
—Quoted in *Maclean's Magazine*, April 1922.

StatScan   Canadian Immigration and Population

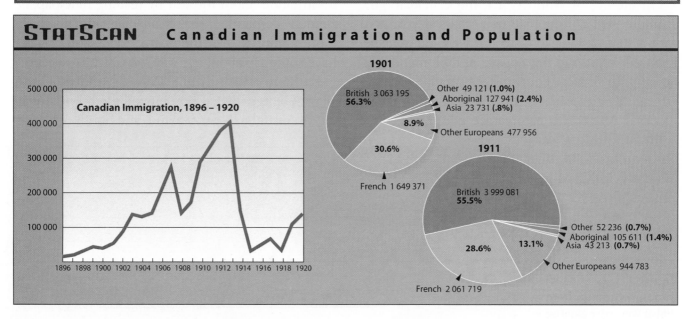

Figure 20-6   Immigrant arrivals in Canada, 1896-1920. Judging by this graph, how successful was Laurier's policy of attracting immigrants to Canada? Why was there an abrupt drop in immigration after 1914?

Figure 20-7   Origins of Canada's population, 1901 and 1911. What are the differences between 1901 and 1911? Does Laurier's immigration policy help explain them?

RECONNECT

1. How does Laurier's immigration policy demonstrate Canada's interdependence with Europe?

2. Why was Clifford Sifton's program to attract immigrants to Canada so successful?

FOCUS

This section will help you understand
a. that Canada's control over its own foreign policy was very limited before World War I
b. that Canada's influence over foreign policy increased as a result of World War I.

On the Eve of World War I

In 1914 Canada was a Dominion, or self-governing member of the British Empire. This meant that Canada controlled its own internal affairs, but that Britain continued to oversee Canada's foreign affairs. If Canada wanted to resolve a problem with another country, it could not do so directly. First, it had to make its wishes known to the British government in London, England. Britain then communicated with the foreign government, and the foreign government had to respond to Britain. Britain then relayed the message to Canada. This sort of arrangement prevented Canada from being treated as an independent country on the world stage.

On the eve of World War I, the Canadian government had a tiny External Affairs department with a staff of 14, two of whom were messengers. External Affairs did not engage in diplomatic relations with other countries. Canada had no embassies or consulates. Instead, the main role of External Affairs was to organize communications with Britain. Its secondary role was to issue passports to Canadian citizens.

Canada and World War I

When Britain declared war on Germany on August 4, 1914, Canada was automatically pulled into the war on the side of Britain. This did not seem remarkable at the time because, outside of Quebec, most Canadians still identified closely with the British Empire. If Britain was under a direct threat from another country, then naturally Canada would come to Britain's aid.

As casualties mounted, Prime Minister Robert Borden insisted that Canada have a larger say in the conduct of the war. Until 1917, the British government did not consult the leaders of the Dominions about strategy and Borden received most of his information about the war by reading newspapers. Borden demanded that Canadian officers have more authority over their own troops and that he have some say about the way the war was waged.

Early in 1917 British Prime Minister David Lloyd-George invited Borden and the prime ministers of Australia, New Zealand, and South Africa, as

Figure 21-1 Canadian troops returning from a drill at Valcartier, Quebec in September 1914, one month after the declaration of war. Canadian Minister of Militia Sir Sam Hughes managed the incredible feat of enlisting, training, equipping, and transporting to England an army of 32 000 soldiers in just over two months.

Figure 21-2 Canadian machine gunners dig in shell holes in the attack on Vimy Ridge in April 1917. In spite of the 3598 troops killed at Vimy Ridge, Canadians at home took great pride in this victory. It sharpened the sense of identity Canadians were beginning to develop. As one soldier who took part in the battle said, "We went up Vimy Ridge as Albertans and Nova Scotians. We came down as Canadians."

Figure 21-3 Major-General Arthur Currie was appointed commander of the Canadian Corps on June 9, 1917.

Passchendaele

By 1917, the war was going very badly for Great Britain and its Allies. Russia fell into a state of civil war and could no longer keep the Germans occupied in the East. In February 1917 Germany announced a policy of unrestricted submarine warfare. The German U-boats were so successful that at one point Britain was reduced to six weeks of supplies. After a French offensive failed in the spring, part of the French army mutinied, refusing to fight any longer.

To relieve the pressure on the Allied front, British General Sir Douglas Haig launched an offensive in July 1917. British and Australian/New Zealand troops suffered heavy casualties in a long, grinding battle that finally bogged down near the Belgian village of Passchendaele. By the time Canadian troops took over in October, months of shelling had destroyed the natural drainage system in the surrounding fields. Autumn rains turned the battlefield into a sea of mud.

By November 7, the Canadians had taken Passchendaele, again succeeding where other troops had failed. It was, however, one of the costliest battles of the war. The Canadian Corps suffered a total of 15 654 dead or wounded, and Prime Minister Borden was furious at the horrific casualties.

well as a representative from India, to London. Along with five members of the British War Cabinet, these leaders formed the new Imperial War Cabinet, which met for the first time on March 2. Suddenly, Canada had a voice in planning the war.

In April 1917, Canadian troops under the command of British General Julian Byng took the previously impregnable Vimy Ridge from German troops. This marked the first time the entire Canadian Corps had fought together as a unit. They captured more territory, prisoners, and guns than any previous British offensive in two-and-a-half years of war. To acknowledge this important victory, Major-General Arthur Currie was appointed the first Canadian commander of the Canadian Corps in June 1917. Canadian troops were finally fighting completely under the command of Canadian officers.

Primary Source

"A SEA OF MUD"

The Passchendaele Campaign was carried on in a sea of mud. I have never seen a drearier sight than the salient in front of Ypres—churned up mud with mucky shell holes and never a tree as far as the eye could reach. It

was necessary to march single file on duck walk because of the mud for a distance of five or six miles when going in for a tour. We were machine-gunned and bombed from the air and subjected to a terrific shelling on the way in and nothing like a real trench system was possible, the line being held by a series of posts in shell holes.

—Letter from Captain Bellenden S. Hutcheson, a World War I veteran, posted on the Veterans Affairs Canada Web site.

Porridge, a ghastly, dreadful porridge, thigh-deep, in which if you got it on the shoulder blade with a bullet that merely knocked you unconscious for two minutes you drowned. We lost lots of men who simply drowned because they were knocked over or stunned and couldn't get recovered before they'd sunk in the mud.

—A World War I veteran in the 4th CMR, in Daniel G. Dancocks, *Legacy of Valour: The Canadians at Passchendaele, 1917* (Edmonton: Hurtig Publishers, 1986), p. 128.

Figure 21-4 Canadian soldiers escort German prisoners and wounded captured at Passchendaele in November 1917. Canadian troops were threatened as much by the mud at Passchendaele as by enemy soldiers. Knowing the risks involved, Major-General Arthur Currie was reluctant to involve the Canadian Corps in the battle. Currie estimated that the Canadian Corps might suffer as many as 16 000 casualties out of 20 000 troops. But pressed by the British generals, Currie finally submitted. In the end Currie's estimate proved accurate.

After the War

When World War I ended in November 1918, Prime Minister Borden insisted that Canada be allowed to send its own representatives to the Versailles Peace Conference instead of being represented by Great Britain. At first Britain was hesitant. In the end, however, Borden's lobbying and Canada's important contributions to the war effort won the day. Canada had spent more than $1 billion on the war effort and had sent 425 000 troops to fight. This was an extraordinary contribution from a country of only eight million people.

Borden signed the Treaty of Versailles on June 28, 1919, marking the first time Canada had exercised this form of **autonomy** from Great Britain. By signing the treaty, Canada also became a member of the new League of Nations. The League made it possible for Canada to interact with the world community as an independent country.

At this point, however, Canada still did not have diplomatic relations with other countries. It had no consulates or embassies. It also did not have the power to negotiate treaties with other countries. Rather, Canada had to negotiate international agreements through the British government in London. Although a beginning had been made, full sovereignty had not yet been achieved.

Figure 21-5 Prime Minister Robert Borden signed the Treaty of Versailles, which formally ends World War I. Before the peace conference, Borden had remarked: "I am beginning to feel that in the end and perhaps sooner than later, Canada must assume full sovereignty. She can give better service to Great Britain and the United States and to the world in that way."

StatScan
Canada in World War I

Total population	8 000 000
Served in armed forces	619 636
Served overseas	425 000
Total armed forces deaths	60 661
Total wounded	172 950

RECONNECT

1. How did Canada's political interdependence with Britain change as a result of World War I?

2. After World War I, in what ways was Canada still dependent on Britain for shaping its foreign policy?

FOCUS

This section will help you understand
   a. to what extent Canada was self-governing at the end of World War I
   b. two steps Canada took to achieve more autonomy during the early 1920s.

Dominion Status

Under the leadership of Prime Minister Robert Borden, Canada made much progress towards carrying out its own foreign affairs during and immediately after World War I. But Canada remained a Dominion and this meant that Britain still retained ultimate control over Canada's foreign affairs. Some Canadians, however, hoped Canada would remain forever under the protection of the British Empire. For example, Arthur Meighen, who succeeded Borden as Conservative prime minister in 1920, wanted to preserve a close connection between Canada and Britain.

Many Canadians, however, felt it was time to cut some of these ties to Britain. They feared that Canada's needs would always take second place to those of Britain. William Lyon Mackenzie King, who came to power in 1921, shared these views.

CaseStudy

THE CHANAK AFFAIR

The first event to test Prime Minister King's belief in Canadian autonomy was the Chanak Affair in 1922. Chanak (now Canakkale) is a small seaport in the Dardanelles, the narrow strait between the Aegean Sea and the Black Sea. According to the Treaty of Versailles that ended World War I, this area was meant to be a neutral zone. The Turkish government under Kemal Ataturk threatened to occupy the area around Chanak. The British government saw this as a threat to its naval supremacy in the region since control of Chanak would give the Turks control over the strait.

Britain immediately asked its Dominions, including Canada, for military support if a war developed with Turkey. In Prime Minister King's opinion, Canada had no direct interest in this faraway conflict. To make matters worse, King first heard about the request through newspaper reports rather than directly from the British government. He considered this a slight to Canada.

Of the British request for military aid, he wrote in his diary: "I confess it annoyed me. It is drafted designedly to play the imperial game, to test out centralization versus autonomy as regards European wars... I do not believe Parliament would sanction the sending of a contingent... I am sure the people of Canada are against participation in this European war." (September 17, 1922).

Figure 22-1 The neutral zone around the Dardanelles, a narrow strait between Europe and Turkey. Because of a war between Turkey and Greece, Turkish leader Kemal Ataturk threatened to occupy Chanak. As a result the Turks might control sea traffic through the Dardanelles.

King's official reply to Britain was that the Canadian Parliament would have to decide whether or not to send Canadian troops. This was a very different response than in 1914 when Canada automatically and unquestioningly joined the British side in World War I. King knew that the Canadian Parliament would most likely vote against Britain's request for military aid, especially since it came so soon after the sacrifices of World War I.

In the end, the Chanak Affair did not erupt into a war between Britain and Turkey. Nevertheless, King had made his point. It was now obvious that British and Canadian interests were not always identical and that Canada was prepared to act independently in such matters.

King believed in Canadian autonomy and took a number of steps towards achieving it.

Not surprisingly, the British point of view was that its Empire would be more powerful if every Dominion followed its lead in foreign policy.

CaseStudy

THE HALIBUT TREATY

Following close on the heels of the Chanak Affair, the Halibut Treaty of 1923 offered Prime Minister King a chance to increase Canada's autonomy by establishing its right to sign treaties independently of Great Britain. American and Canadian officials had successfully negotiated the fishing season for halibut in the North Pacific. Such a treaty was of no direct concern to Britain.

King decided this was the perfect opportunity to set a **precedent** for excluding Britain from the treaty process. He informed London that the Canadian Minister of Fisheries, Ernest Lapointe, would sign the treaty with the U.S. by himself. Contrary to tradition, King did not call on the British ambassador in Washington to sign the treaty on behalf of Canada. Britain was alarmed, but King got his way. In this way a treaty over fishing rights became one of the landmarks along Canada's drive to autonomy.

Later in 1923, Britain called all its Dominions to London for an Imperial Conference. The Dominions passed a resolution endorsing Canada's treaty-making process. After this Britain officially granted all its Dominions the right to make their own treaties with foreign countries.

Figure 22-2 Prime Minister King on board the Montcalm on the way to the Imperial Conference in 1923. King believed Canada should control its foreign affairs independently of Great Britain.

Primary Source

"THE SIGNATURE OF THE CANADIAN MINISTER SHOULD BE SUFFICIENT."

"When the British government learned of Canada's plans to sign the Halibut Treaty on its own, the British ambassador to the U.S. sent a cable to Prime Minister King. Britain demanded that its representative in Washington D.C. also be allowed to sign the treaty."

—Canadian Minister of Fisheries Ernest Lapointe.

"I have been instructed by His Majesty's Government to sign [the] Treaty in association with Mr. Lapointe."

—British Ambassador to the U.S., Sir Auckland Geddes in a cable to the Canadian government, February 12, 1923.

King waited a week and then curtly informed the British government its representative was not wanted at the treaty signing.

"The view of my Ministers…is that the Treaty being one of concern solely to Canada and the United States, and not affecting in particular any imperial interest, the signature of the Canadian Minister should be sufficient, and they would respectfully request that His Majesty's Ambassador at Washington be instructed accordingly."

—King's reply on February 28, 1923.

RECONNECT

1. How did the Chanak Affair and the Halibut Treaty advance Canada's drive for complete independence from Great Britain? Be specific in your reply.

FOCUS

This section will help you understand
a. how Canada achieved autonomy from Great Britain
b. what autonomy means to Canada.

Autonomy or Independence?

The final steps in Canada's march to achieve complete independence from Britain occurred from 1926 to 1931. The word "independence," however, was rarely heard when Canadian and British leaders spoke in public. Prime Minister King wanted to avoid the slightest suggestion that achieving Canadian independence was in any way similar to the War of American Independence that gave birth to the United States. Instead King and other Canadian leaders preferred to use the word "autonomy." Whatever the label, this drive for a new kind of relationship with Britain represented a major break with the past.

CaseStudy

THE KING-BYNG CRISIS

Today the governor general is the representative of the British monarch in Canada. At the beginning of the 20th century, Britain regarded the governor general not only as the symbolic head of state, but also as an active agent of the British government. If the Canadian prime minister wanted to contact the British prime minister or the American president, he could do so only through the governor general.

When Prime Minister Mackenzie King wanted to dissolve Parliament and call an election in June 1926, the governor general's role became a controversial issue. The normal course was for the governor general to grant the prime minister's request to dissolve Parliament automatically. King, however, headed a **minority government** that was in danger of losing an important vote in the House of Commons. As well, King had called an election only eight months before.

Governor General Julian Byng refused King's request. When King resigned, Byng invited Conservative leader Arthur Meighen to form the government. Meighen agreed, but his government fell on a vote of no-confidence after only three days in power. Byng then had no choice but to call an election.

During the campaign that followed, King posed the following question to the voters: Should the governor general follow the requests of the Canadian prime minister, or should he be allowed to act independently? King wanted Canadians to see a strong and independent governor general as a relic or hold-over from the British Empire. He argued that the governor general should be nothing more than a symbolic head of state who takes orders from the real authority, the Canadian House of Commons.

King's Liberals won a convincing victory in the 1926 election. King took this as a sign that the majority of Canadians supported his stand on the need for a governor general with no real authority.

Figure 23-1 Mackenzie King, on the campaign trail in Vancouver in 1926, buys a raffle ticket from a World War I veteran.

Figure 23-2 Governor General Julian Byng. Byng was commander of the Canadian Corps when it captured Vimy Ridge in 1917. He served as governor general from 1921 to 1926.

Canadian Federal Elections Results, 1925 and 1926		
Party	1925	1926
Liberal	99	128
Conservative	116	91
Progressive	24	20
Independent	6	6

Figure 23-3 How do these election results reflect the success of Mackenzie King's campaign strategy?

The Statute of Westminster

In 1926 leaders of the Dominions and Britain met in London, England. Prime Minister King was a key participant at this conference. This meeting, like others held since the end of World War I, was called an Imperial Conference. The Dominion countries were still considered members of the British Empire at this time. The 1926 Imperial Conference made a number of recommendations that, in effect, put an end to Canada's inferior status under the authority of the British Empire. Many traditions of the British Empire continued, but often in name only. For example, meetings of all Dominion countries continued to be called Imperial Conferences until the last one in 1937.

These recommendations were summarized in a document called the Balfour Report. Canada and the other dominions were to enjoy a status equal to that of Great Britain. From this point forward, they would no longer be called the British Empire but the Commonwealth of Nations.

On December 11, 1931, five years after the 1926 Imperial Conference, the British Parliament passed the Statute of Westminster. This statute gave the main recommendations in the Balfour Report the force of law. For Canada, the practical results were:
▶ from this time forward Canada had the right to pass any laws it desired, whether or not they conflicted with British law.

Primary Source
"I DID NOT LIKE THE WORD 'INDEPENDENT.'"

In 1926 Mackenzie King met General J.B.M. Hertzog, the prime minister of South Africa, at the Imperial Conference in London, England. When Hertzog used the term "independent" to describe the political condition he wished for South Africa and other Dominions, King reacted with alarm. The following quotation is an excerpt from his diary for October 27, 1926.

"I told him I did not like the word 'independent,' and [that] anything like a declaration of independence would not be understood in Canada in the sense in which he meant it; it would be looked upon as a parallel to [the Declaration of Independence] of 1776 of the United States."

—C.P. Stacey, *Canada and the Age of Conflict* (Toronto: Oxford University Press, 1981), p. 86.

Primary Source
THE BALFOUR REPORT

"They [the Dominions] are autonomous Communities within the British Empire, equal in status, in no way subordinate one to another in any aspect of their domestic or external affairs, though united by a common allegiance to the Crown, and freely associated as members of the British Commonwealth of Nations."

—Excerpt from *The Balfour Report*, 1926.

▶ the governor general was no longer to be an agent of Britain, but simply the symbolic head of state.
▶ the Canadian prime minister was officially authorized to communicate directly with the British government or with the heads of any other government.

The passage of the Statute of Westminster was the beginning of full autonomy for Canada.

RECONNECT

1. How did Canada achieve full autonomy from Great Britain?

2. How did Canada's achievement of autonomy differ from the United States' achievement of independence from Great Britain?

Canada's European War

Canada did not participate in any of the political maneuvering in Europe that led up to Germany's invasion of Poland on September 1, 1939. When Great Britain declared war on Germany two days later, Canada did not automatically join the British side as in 1914. Instead Prime Minister Mackenzie King insisted that only Parliament could decide whether or not Canada was at war with Germany. It was only after a debate, and an unrecorded vote in the House of Commons, that the Canadian government declared war on Germany, a week after Britain.

After France's defeat in June 1940, and until both the Soviet Union and the U.S. entered the war in 1941, Canada was Britain's most important ally. Canadian support became crucial after the fall of France, when Britain faced Nazi Germany alone across the English Channel. To support the war effort Canada transformed its economy and created an impressive military machine. But King himself dealt mostly with domestic problems, such as the troublesome issue of **conscription**. In regard to the strategy and planning of the war, he was usually content to follow the lead of Britain and the United States.

Figure 24-1 Prime Minister Mackenzie King, Prime Minister Winston Churchill, and President Franklin Roosevelt at the Quebec Conference in 1943. Although King was the host of this conference, he was not invited to participate in the discussions between Churchill and Roosevelt on the planning of the war. In light of this, is the photograph misleading in any way? Explain.

Primary Source

"A NIGHTMARE AND SHEER MADNESS."

In 1937, when the possibility of war with Germany still seemed distant, Mackenzie King did not hesitate to pledge Canadian military aid to Great Britain.

"If Germany should ever turn her mind from constructive to destructive efforts against the United Kingdom, all the Dominions would come to her aid and…there would be great numbers of Canadians anxious to swim the Atlantic!"

—Prime Minister Mackenzie King at an Imperial Conference, June 16, 1937.

Five months before the outbreak of the war, King sensed the voters' reluctance to support another full-scale effort only 20 years after the immense sacrifices of World War I. His statements reflected his belief that Canada would most likely come to the aid of Britain in a war, but the effort would need to be scaled down. If casualties could be kept well below the level of World War I, then Canada would remain a united country.

"The idea that every 20 years this country should automatically and as a matter of course take part in a war overseas for democracy or self-determination of other small nations…and to these ends to risk the lives of its people, risk bankruptcy and political disunion, seems to many a nightmare and sheer madness."

—Prime Minister Mackenzie King in the House of Commons, March 30, 1939.

Supporting the War Effort

Through its army, air force, and navy, Canada was a major source of support for Great Britain in the dark days after the fall of France in 1940.

Canada also played a very important role in relieving the desperate economic situation of Britain, which was reeling under the strain of paying for its war effort. In January 1942, Canada announced what came to be called "The Billion Dollar Gift," an outright donation of $1 billion to Great Britain. This gift was accompanied by another $700 million in interest-free loans. The British used these funds to purchase weapons and other war supplies manufactured in Canada.

When these funds ran out, they were replaced by a program of Mutual Aid that provided $2 billion in supplies at no charge to the Allies, with most of the supplies going to Britain. In all, Britain received more than $3 billion in financial help from Canada during the war.

The Outcome of the War

It is ironic that Canada's financial support of Britain during World War II resulted in a decrease in Canadian-British interdependence. First, Canada emerged from the war as a **middle power** with the fourth-largest air force and third-largest navy in the world. Second, Canada made wartime agreements with the U.S. that resulted in close economic and military cooperation. Third, Britain came out of the war a much weaker country than in 1939, and with debts that would cripple its economy for years to come. All these factors pushed Canada to develop

Figure 24-2 A convoy of Canadian ships in Bedford Basin, Halifax carry war supplies for Great Britain.

Primary Source
"HOW LARGE THIS CANADIAN ASSISTANCE IS."

"We should like to emphasise how large this Canadian assistance is. Canada has a relatively small population, only about $11\frac{1}{2}$ millions as against over 130 millions in the United States …She is giving away goods to the value of nearly one-quarter of her budget expenditure, whereas lend-lease assistance by the United States to all countries has been running recently at about one-eighth of *her* budget expenditure…Canada is not only devoting as large a proportion of her national income to defence expenditure as any other country, but…the proportion of the defence expenditure which is given away in the form of free supplies is higher in Canada than in any other country."

—From a memo distributed by a British cabinet minister to the British cabinet in February 1943.

closer ties with its southern neighbour—the American superpower.

StatScan   Canada Before and After the War

	1939	1945
Population	11 267 000 million	12 027 000 million
Gross National Product*	$5.6 billion	$11.8 billion
Government Spending	$680 million	$5.1 billion
Income Taxes Collected	$112 million	$809 million
No. of Federal Government Workers	46 106	115 908

*A country's gross national product is the value of all the goods and services it produces in one year, plus its return on foreign investments.

RECONNECT

1. In what ways did Canada grow during World War II?

2. How did Canada's relationship with Britain change during the war?

FOCUS

This section will help you understand
- a. Canada's role within several international organizations
- b. the ways in which these organizations have contributed to globalization.

Canada and the United Nations

Considering its status as a middle power, Canada has played an unusually prominent role in the United Nations since this organization was founded in 1945. The Following is a partial list of some of Canada's accomplishments within this international organization:

▶ Canada is a "charter member" of the UN, one of the 50 original members that signed the UN Charter on June 26, 1945.

▶ A Canadian law professor at McGill University, John Humphrey, drew up the UN's Universal Declaration of Human Rights. Humphrey also served for 20 years as the director of the UN's Division of Human Rights.

▶ Canada has been elected to a record six two-year terms on the Security Council, the chief decision-making body of the UN. Canada's most recent term will run from 1999 through 2000.

▶ In 1956, future Canadian Prime Minister Lester Pearson was the first person to propose a UN **peacekeeping** mission to solve an international crisis. Pearson offered the idea of a peacekeeping force made up of soldiers from several different countries as a solution to the **Suez Crisis**. The idea helped to bring an end to the conflict between England and France and Egypt. For his efforts, Pearson won the Nobel Peace Prize in 1957.

▶ Since 1956, Canada has participated in over 40 peacekeeping missions, more than any other member of the UN.

In general, Canada's participation in the UN has greatly enhanced its role in world affairs, which was minimal before World War II.

Canada is also a member of two powerful organizations that are connected with the UN: the World Bank and the International Monetary Fund. Both of these organizations have had a major impact on globalization by controlling the flow of money among countries around the world.

Figure 25-1   Canadian peacekeeping troops on patrol in the western Bosnian town of Dr Var in 1998. Canada has provided troops for more peacekeeping missions than any other UN member country, and 102 Canadian soldiers have been killed while on these missions. The UN prefers to draw its peacekeeping troops from middle power countries like Canada rather than from superpowers like the U.S. Why do you think this is?

The World Bank

The World Bank is an agency of the UN that first began operating in 1945. Its offices are in Washington, D.C. Originally the purpose of the World Bank was to help countries that had been devastated by World War II. Today, its major purpose is to provide money for projects that will help in the economic development of member nations.

Originally, the Bank concentrated on funding large-scale projects such as hydroelectric dams, water-supply lines, and roads. Today the typical project funded by the World Bank involves farm improvements or other developments in rural areas. The World Bank has also provided loans to Asia Pacific countries to help them cope with the economic downturn which began in 1997.

Most of the money the World Bank lends to needy countries comes from "subscriptions" paid by its members. Each country that belongs to the World Bank pays an annual fee, which is based on the size of that country's economy.

Figure 25-2 In Dinujpur, Bangladesh vegetable gardening skills are taught to help women become self-sufficient. This project was funded by the World Bank.

PROFILE		
	World Bank	**IMF**
Headquarters	Washington D.C.	Washington D.C.
Membership	181 countries	182 countries
Staff	8 468	2 600
Budget 1997	$U.S. 20 billion loaned to countries in need	$U.S. 195 billion collected from member countries

The International Monetary Fund

Like the World Bank, the International Monetary Fund (IMF) began operating in 1945 and is an agency of the UN with its headquarters in Washington, D.C. The role of the IMF is to

▶ stabilize **exchange rates** for currencies around the world, and

▶ promote international trade among member nations.

In 1998 there were at least 162 different currencies. For countries to conduct business with each other, they must be able to convert these currencies. For example, if a Canadian company wants to import Japanese cameras, it must pay the Japanese company in yen—the Japanese currency. The IMF pushes for convertible currencies which means that they can easily be bought and sold. It also promotes a system of flexible currency exchange rates so that a country's currency tends to fall and rise with its economic performance.

Most of the world's governments have different levels of debt which must be paid off from their yearly budgets. Many countries, including Canada owe money to foreign banks. Usually these debts must be paid off in U.S. dollars which is the world standard. When a country's currency loses value, these loans become more expensive to pay off. Suddenly a country might have problems making its loan payments. This is called a balance of payments problem.

Since a bankrupt country would be an economic catastrophe for its citizens, and perhaps disrupt the global economy, a temporary solution is for the

NETSURFER

THE IMF AND WORLD BANK

Historical, statistical as well as other detailed information on many projects and activities of the IMF and World Bank is available at the following Web sites.

http://www.imf.org
http://www.worldbank.org

IMF to step in and offer a loan. To receive a loan a country must usually guarantee that it will reform its economy so that it will not face the same problems again. The IMF has no direct power to enforce changes in these countries, but the threat of withholding money already committed by the IMF is often very persuasive to countries on the brink of bankruptcy.

As with the World Bank, much of the IMF's operating funds come from subscriptions paid by member countries, both in their own currencies and in gold **bullion**. Countries such as the U.S., Japan, and Germany pay much larger subscriptions than countries such as Guatemala, Somalia, and Vietnam because their economies are much larger. However, countries that pay larger fees also have greater voting powers. In fact, the U.S., Japan, and Germany by themselves can out-vote the other 179 members of the International Monetary Fund! If they chose to cooperate, these three countries could completely control the flow of IMF funds around the world.

CaseStudy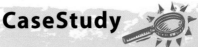

DOES IMF STAND FOR "IMPOSING MISERY AND FAMINE?"

Since its founding in 1945, the International Monetary Fund has been a big help to the cause of worldwide economic stability. At the same time, it has become an unpopular institution in some countries. The fund has no control over nations with a surplus in their balance of payments, but it does have authority over nations that owe it money. This means that the IMF is frequently in conflict with developing countries, the very nations that are most likely to have problems with their balance of payments.

In return for rescheduling debt payments, the IMF will often impose what it calls "Structural Adjustment" programs on debtor nations. These programs usually force the countries to cut spending on things like welfare and housing services and to slash public payrolls by laying off government workers. The money saved goes to help pay off the countries' international debts. Cuts like these can mean great hardships for the people in the countries involved. This is why in some African countries, IMF is said to stand for "Imposing Misery and Famine."

—Adapted from Stuart Corbridge, ed., *World Economy* (New York: Oxford University Press, 1993), p.27.

Figure 25-3   An Indonesian student shouts anti-International Monetary Fund slogans at a protest outside the Finance Ministry in Jakarta in January 1998. The sign reads, "The IMF is the agent of capitalist countries."

The Commonwealth of Nations

In addition to the United Nations, Canada belongs to several other organizations with international connections. One of the most important of these is the Commonwealth of Nations. The Commonwealth consists of 53 member countries, all of which were once part of the British Empire.

Canada has played a prominent role in the modern Commonwealth which has transformed itself significantly since the end of World War II. In 1949, the word "British" was dropped from the official title. The organization has been known since then simply as the Commonwealth of Nations to emphasize the equality of all member countries. In 1965, the Commonwealth established its first permanent headquarters in London headed by a secretary-general. The first secretary-general of the Commonwealth was a Canadian, Arnold Smith, who served in that role for 10 years.

The leaders of Commonwealth countries meet every two years to discuss economic, political, and social issues. All member countries have an equal say at these meetings. Although the Commonwealth is loosely organized with no formal constitution, member countries have approved declarations of principle from time to time. They have also united to condemn fellow member countries whose policies violated the Commonwealth ideals of democra-

Primary Source
IS THE COMMONWEALTH WORTH IT?

To some extent, our Commonwealth membership gives us a place in world councils that is denied to the United States. And because we have no axe to grind and harbour no territorial ambitions, past or present, our influence in Commonwealth proceedings can be useful and impressive…The Commonwealth is a forum where white and black can meet and talk together as equals and where they can often agree to compromise. As long as it can be useful in these ways, it is an institution that is well worth preserving.

—Former Canadian Finance Minister Walter Gordon, 1966.

Primary Source
"WE WERE OPPOSED TO RACIAL DISCRIMINATION."

Speaking for Canada…I pointed out that we were opposed to racial discrimination, and made it clear that I could not approve any formula or solution which did not maintain beyond any doubt that non-discrimination in respect of race and colour is an essential principle of the Commonwealth association.

—Prime Minister John Diefenbaker in his report to the House of Commons on the Commonwealth meeting in London, 1961.

cy, human rights, racial equality, and **sustainable development.**

CaseStudy

CANADA AND HUMAN RIGHTS
ISSUES IN THE COMMONWEALTH

At the Commonwealth Conference in London in 1961, Canadian Prime Minister John Diefenbaker took a stand as a strong advocate of racial equality. Diefenbaker openly criticized the government of Commonwealth member South Africa for its policy of **apartheid.** This policy discriminated against all non-white residents of South Africa, who together made up 80% of the population. These people had no voting rights and could live only in designated areas. Schools and hospitals were also racially segregated.

Diefenbaker sided with the African and Asian countries that wanted to take a tougher stand against South Africa. Britain, Australia, and New Zealand were unwilling to criticize South Africa. After intense criticism from Diefenbaker, South Africa withdrew from the Commonwealth in 1961. It was not readmitted until 1991 when black leader Nelson Mandela was elected president.

In 1994, Canada joined other Commonwealth countries in condemning the dictatorship in Nigeria. After the Nigerian government executed nine political activists, the country was expelled from the Commonwealth.

La Francophonie

The roots of la Francophonie go back to 1969 when 20 French-speaking countries met in Niamey, Niger in Africa. This conference outlined the structure for the 1970 founding of the Agency for Cultural and Technical Cooperation (ACCT), which is the cornerstone of la Francophonie. It promotes closer ties among French-speaking countries by encouraging cooperation in education, culture, and technology.

In 1986, the first la Francophonie summit meeting was held in Paris, with leaders from 41 countries participating. Since then summit meetings have been held on average every two years. They have become a major forum for discussing issues important to French-speaking countries around the world.

Canada's Role in la Francophonie

Canada's background as a bilingual country with two official languages has strongly influenced its participation in la Francophonie. The Canadian provinces of Quebec and New Brunswick are represented at la Francophonie summits by their premiers. They have observer status and participate in cultural issues.

Figure 25-4 Canada Post issued this stamp on March 20, 1995 to commemorate the 25th anniversary of the ACCT.

Canada has also pushed la Francophonie to become more involved in human rights issues. So far, however, la Francophonie has hesitated to criticize countries that violate human rights. Delegates to the 1995 summit for example, could only agree to a weak statement regarding the massacre of hundreds of thousands of people in Rwanda and Burundi, and the execution of opposition leaders by the military dictatorship in Nigeria.

RECONNECT

1. In what ways has Canada contributed to international organizations such as the United Nations, the Commonwealth, and la Francophonie?

2. What benefits has Canada enjoyed through its membership in these organizations?

FOCUS

This section will help you understand
  a. what the European Union is and how it was created
  b. the economic and political relationships between Canada and the European Union.

What is the European Union?

The European Union (EU) is an association of European countries designed to strengthen the political and economic links among its members. As of 1998 15 countries, with a total population of 372 million people, belonged to the European Union, making it the world's largest multi-country market. Within the European Union, people, products, and services can pass freely from one country to another. People do not need visas, and goods are not subject to duties or other taxes as they pass between countries.

Since restrictions are minimal, and visitors are usually not required to show identification papers at border crossings, all EU countries must maintain a higher level of security over travellers entering from outside the EU.

The EU is expected to grow even larger by extending membership to other countries in Europe, especially in eastern Europe. As well, the level of interdependence among the member countries will also increase over the years. For example, a common European currency called the "euro" is scheduled to replace the various local currencies by July 1, 2002.

TIMELINE ⟋⟍ The European Union

1951 — France, West Germany, Belgium, Luxembourg, the Netherlands, and Italy form the European Coal and Steel Community in order to insure adequate resources for their industries in the aftermath of World War II.

1958 — The same six countries sign the Treaty of Rome, establishing the European Economic Community (EEC).

1963 — French President Charles de Gaulle vetoes British membership in the EEC because of his suspicions about the close relations between Britain and the U.S. He felt that Britain was not European enough to join the EEC.

1965 — The Brussels Treaty merges several European organizations, including the EEC into the European Community (EC).

1968 — The EC eliminates all tariffs between member countries, lowering prices for trade goods. The EC becomes a great economic success.

1973 — Great Britain, Ireland, and Denmark join the EC. Britain's entry means it will focus its economic activities more on the EC than on Canada.

1979 — The first direct elections to the European Parliament.

1981 — Greece joins the EC.

1986 — Spain and Portugal join the EC.

1987 — The EC passes the Single European Act. By 1992, this act will create a single free trade market with no customs checks at border crossings.

1992 — The Treaty of European Unity, signed in Maastricht, Belgium passes into law. It is designed to provide a central banking system, a common currency, and an expanded role in foreign policy for a united Europe. The 12 member countries are now to be called the European Union.

1995 — The EU decides that the new European currency will be called the "euro" and used at first in banking transactions on January 1, 1999. Austria, Finland, and Sweden join the EU bringing the number up to 15 countries.

1997 — Poland, Hungary, the Czech Republic, Slovenia, Estonia, and Cyprus pass the first hurdle towards becoming EU members by 2004.

MapStudy — THE EUROPEAN UNION IN 1998

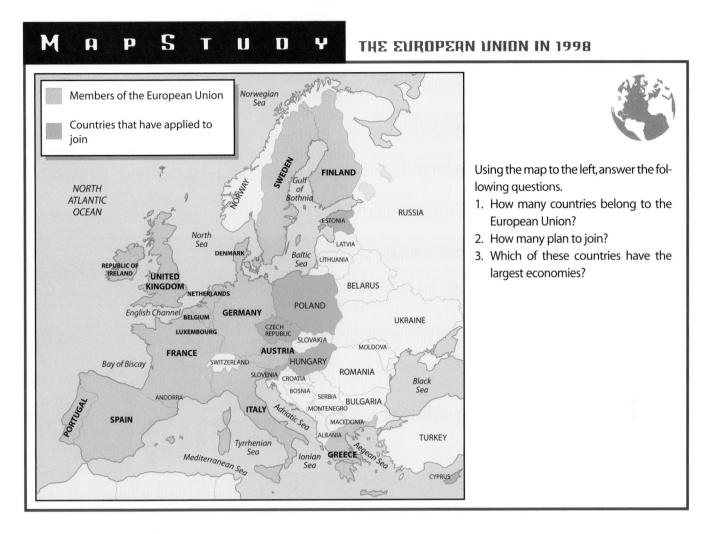

Members of the European Union

Countries that have applied to join

Using the map to the left, answer the following questions.

1. How many countries belong to the European Union?
2. How many plan to join?
3. Which of these countries have the largest economies?

Institutions of the European Union

The European Union is more than a huge marketplace. It has formed several institutions that have resulted in closer political cooperation among the countries of Europe. Four of these institutions are described below.

The Council of Ministers

Located in Brussels, Belgium, the Council of Ministers is the most important decision-making body in the EU. Various cabinet ministers from member countries, for example agricultural ministers and finance ministers, can meet here to discuss problems in their special areas. The most important meetings take place twice a year and are attended by the heads of government of the different member countries. The meeting of this group of government leaders is known as the European Council.

The European Commission

The European Commission is located in Brussels, Belgium. It has 20 commissioners chosen from the 15 EU countries; one commissioner is selected as president. All commissioners and the president are appointed for a six-year term. Like cabinet ministers, each commissioner has an area of expertise and can propose legislation.

The European Parliament

The European Parliament is located in Strasbourg, France. The Parliament has limited law making powers but must approve proposed legislation from the European Commission. It has 626 members called Members of the European Parliament (MEPs) who are elected in their member countries every five years. The number of MEPs each country can elect is based on the size of that country's population. The European Parliament must also approve the annual EU budget.

The European Court of Justice

The European Court of Justice has 15 judges who are appointed to six year terms by the Council of Ministers. Located in Luxembourg, the court upholds EU laws and treaties and resolves disputes among member countries.

Canada's Relations with the EU

The most important links between Canada and the EU are trade and investment. The EU is Canada's second-largest trading partner after the U.S. In 1996, about 7% of all Canada's exports went to the EU; these exports were worth approximately $14.86 billion. In the same year Canada imported about $22.73 billion worth of goods from the EU.

In regard to investment, the EU is also Canada's second-largest source of foreign investment. Investment from EU countries more than doubled from 1985 to 1995. One indicator of the importance of investment from EU countries is that they invested more than five times as much as Japan did in 1995.

But there are dangers to Canada's close relationship with the European Union. Read the primary source on this page and the case study on page 87.

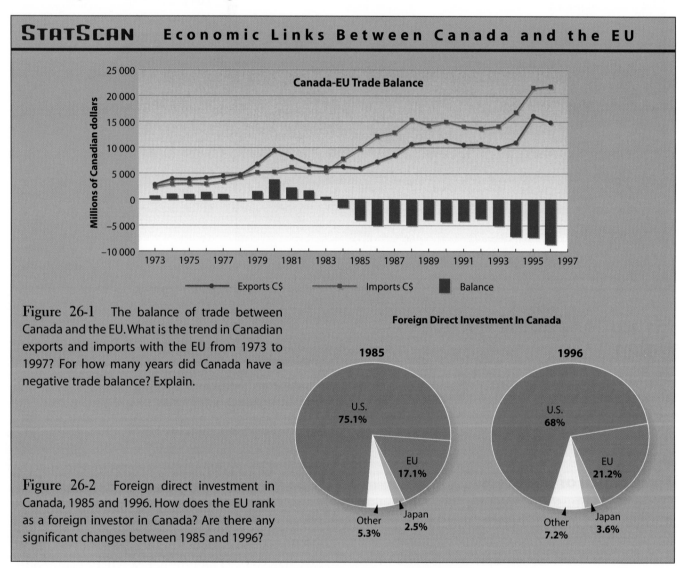

StatScan Economic Links Between Canada and the EU

Canada-EU Trade Balance

— Exports C$ — Imports C$ ■ Balance

Figure 26-1 The balance of trade between Canada and the EU. What is the trend in Canadian exports and imports with the EU from 1973 to 1997? For how many years did Canada have a negative trade balance? Explain.

Foreign Direct Investment In Canada

1985
U.S. 75.1%
EU 17.1%
Japan 2.5%
Other 5.3%

1996
U.S. 68%
EU 21.2%
Japan 3.6%
Other 7.2%

Figure 26-2 Foreign direct investment in Canada, 1985 and 1996. How does the EU rank as a foreign investor in Canada? Are there any significant changes between 1985 and 1996?

Primary Source

A DANGER IN THE CANADA-EU RELATIONSHIP

Canada's relations with the EU can easily be held hostage to a dispute over a single issue involving primarily the interests of one member state. In such cases, a problem with one member country automatically translates into a problem with the entire Union... A medium-sized country, such as Canada, is at a decided disadvantage in dealing with a large bloc of countries like the EU. Moreover, the EU's economic and political leverage will grow in relation to that of Canada as the Union absorbs up to 13 more countries. The growing imbalance of power will place Canada in an increasingly disadvantageous bargaining position.

—From a Canadian Senate report, *European Integration: The Implications for Canada,* (1996).

CaseStudy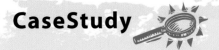

THE TURBOT WAR

The so-called Turbot War that took place in 1995 between Spain and Canada revealed a danger in Canada's relations with the EU. Turbot is a highly prized flatfish that frequents the Grand Banks off Newfoundland. The Canadian government felt fish stocks on the Grand Banks were at such a low level that the entire fishery was faced with catastrophe. The government first reduced quotas for fishers within the 200-mile limit from Canadian shores, and Minister of Fisheries Brian Tobin then tried to negotiate a reduction of EU fishing on the Grand Banks in international waters. Tobin claimed that fishing by EU countries, especially Spain, was depleting turbot stocks to the point that they might not ever recover.

When Spanish trawlers continued to fish just outside the 200-mile limit, Tobin ordered Canadian fisheries patrol boats to seize one of the ships. On March 9, 1995, a patrol boat fired shots across the bow of the Spanish trawler *Estai* and then seized the fishing boat and arrested the crew. This enraged Spanish leaders who immediately took their case to the EU.

For Canada, which was negotiating a wide-ranging trade and political agreement with the EU, the timing of the Turbot War was unfortunate. Canada wanted an agreement similar to the one that the U.S. had just signed with the EU. Spain was able to use its influence inside the EU to sidetrack the Canadian agreement for 18 months. While the Joint Canada-EU Action Plan was finally signed in 1996, this episode showed how a disagreement with one European country could damage relations with the entire EU.

Figure 26-3 The Spanish trawler *Estai* comes into St. John's. The seizure of the *Estai* in 1995 crippled relations between Canada and Spain and threatened to derail an important agreement between Canada and the EU.

NΣTSURFΣR

EUROPEAN UNION

1. Detailed information on the EU can be found at its Web site:
   http://europa.eu.int
   This information includes:
   - historical background
   - description of the EU's many institutions
   - lists of member countries
   - summaries of long-range plans.

2. Information on Canada's relationship with the EU can be found at the Web site for the Canadian Department of Foreign Affairs and International Trade:
   http://www.dfait-maeci.gc.ca
   Once into the Web site, the user must link to Europe under "Foreign Policy."

Figure 26-4 This is the home page of the European Union. Information is available in 10 of the 11 different languages spoken in EU countries.

RECONNECT

1. Describe the historical background of the formation of the EU.

2. In what way has the EU changed Canada's relationship with European countries? Explain.

FOCUS

This section will help you understand
a. in what ways globalization has changed the world
b. the challenges globalization presents to Canadian sovereignty.

Globalization and Canada

The world's economy has experienced a dramatic shift in the latter half of the 20th century. Economic links among nations and peoples around the world have steadily multiplied. This growth in worldwide trade and investment is often referred to as globalization. Canada's global economic links determine the way a growing number of Canadians make their living. The key features of this globalized economy are:

▶ rapid advances in high-tech communications, such as the development of computer technology which made the Internet a reality.

▶ the reduction of global trade barriers. This happens through agreements like NAFTA and the EU which eliminate tariffs.

▶ an increasing share of the world's economy devoted to trade among countries. Trade increased its share of the world economy from 7% to 22% between 1950 and 1997.

▶ trade increasingly taking place across international borders, but within the branches of multinational corporations. About two-thirds of world trade now takes place this way.

▶ a dramatic increase in foreign investments. Multinational corporations have expanded their investments around the world. Between 1987 and 1997, these assets increased three-fold to a remarkable $3 trillion.

Globalization poses many challenges to countries like Canada. With the growth of the global economy, multinational corporations will increase in size and influence. Since most multinational corporations are not based in Canada, this means that the leaders of foreign-owned corporations may have an even greater deal of influence over the lives of Canadians in the future.

Will globalization threaten Canada's sovereignty? Will the ability of Canadian citizens to participate in their government's decision-making process diminish? Canadians must face these important questions as we enter the 21st century.

Profile: General Motors

The American multinational, General Motors, is a good example of a corporation that has an important economic presence in many countries. The following is a General Motors profile.

Founded in 1908, General Motors has grown into the world's largest industrial corporation and full-line vehicle manufacturer. In 1996, the company employed over 647 000 people and partnered with over 30 000 companies worldwide. As the largest U.S. exporter of cars and trucks, and having manufacturing, assembly, or component operations in 50 countries, General Motors has a global presence in over 190 countries.

Along with designing, manufacturing, and marketing of vehicles, General Motors has interests in telecommunications and space, aerospace and defence, consumer and automotive systems, and heavy-duty automatic transmissions.
—General Motors Web site www.gm.com

Figure 27-1 The 73-storey Renaissance Center in Detroit, Michigan serves as the headquarters of General Motors. In which way is GM a global corporation? Why can a multinational corporation like GM often obtain favourable treatment, such as tax breaks, when building factories in foreign countries?

International Treaties and Globalization

Several treaties and agreements have attempted to smooth the transition to a global economy. We have already seen how the European Union, the Asia-Pacific Economic Co-operation, and the North America Free Trade Agreement make it easier for corporations to trade and invest across the borders of member countries.

Two other treaties have been designed to lower trade barriers on a global rather than a regional basis. They promise to have a major impact on the trend towards globalization.

▶ The World Trade Organization (WTO), formerly known as the General Agreement on Tariffs and Trade, came into existence in 1994. Its goal is to increase global trade and economic development by eliminating tariffs and other laws that restrict the free passage of goods from one country to another. It has already influenced decisions made by the Canadian government.

▶ The Multilateral Agreement on Investment (MAI) is a highly controversial agreement that has been under discussion since 1995. It is designed to establish a single set of rules that will govern investment around the world. Under the MAI, a multinational corporation that feels it has been unfairly treated by a country's government would be able to sue in an international court administered by the MAI.

After the negotiating countries failed to reach an agreement in 1998, it was not clear whether the MAI would ever be approved. There is still a desire by many countries in the world, supported by the largest multinational corporations, to pass something like it eventually.

CaseStudy

SPORTS ILLUSTRATED VS. THE CANADIAN GOVERNMENT

The WTO's decision in a case pitting the American magazine *Sports Illustrated* against the Canadian government illustrates how treaties like NAFTA and organizations like the WTO can have a strong impact on Canadian culture.

The Dispute
In 1997, the American publishers of *Sports Illustrated* complained to the WTO that the Canadian government was treating them unfairly. In this case *Sports Illustrated* had already appealed unsuccessfully to a tribunal under the terms of NAFTA. The NAFTA tribunal had decided that the actions taken by the Canadian government against *Sports Illustrated* were allowable under provisions designed to protect culture. All this occurred after Canada had slapped a high tax on the magazine's Canadian edition. The government claimed that *Sports Illustrated* was charging such low rates that Canadian magazines could not hope to compete with it.

　　The Canadian edition of *Sports Illustrated* had exactly the same content as the American edition but with Canadian advertisements. The American editors of *Sports Illustrated* transferred their stories electronically from their headquarters in the U.S. to Canada, where the Canadian edition was printed. The magazine hired virtually no Canadian writers or editors. *Sports Illustrated* could easily undercut prices charged by Canadian magazines because it already made a healthy profit in the huge American market. In the meantime, Canadian magazines had to charge higher advertising rates in order to cover their costs in a much smaller market.

Figure 27-2 The Canadian edition of magazines like *Sports Illustrated* usually have very little Canadian content. Canadian publishers argue that by attracting Canadian advertising dollars while spending most of their editorial dollars in the U.S., they threaten Canada's magazine industry.

The Outcome
The WTO decided in favour of *Sports Illustrated* and instructed the Canadian government to drop the special tax on American magazines. According to the WTO, both American and Canadian magazines should be treated equally in the Canadian market. After the WTO's decision, Canadian magazine publishers complained they would go broke without government support. Without financial aid, they pointed out, Canadians would soon have only American magazines to read. In the end, this would weaken Canadian culture.

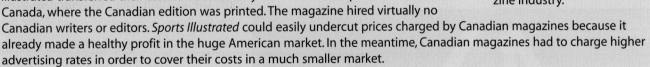

RECONNECT

1. How has globalization affected Canada economically and culturally?

2. Do you think globalization is a threat to Canadian sovereignty? Defend your answer.

FOCUS

This section will help you understand
a. how global warming will affect Canada
b. what steps Canada and other countries are taking to prevent global warming.

Greenhouse Gases and Global Climate Change

Global warming can be defined as a gradual rise in the Earth's average temperature. This is actually part of a natural process called the **greenhouse effect**, which is caused by a build-up of gases in the Earth's atmosphere. Greenhouse gases like carbon dioxide (CO_2) rise into the Earth's atmosphere and create a gaseous layer that traps some of the heat from the sun instead of releasing it into space. Without this greenhouse effect, the Earth would not stay warm enough to sustain life.

Trouble develops, however, when the greenhouse gases build up to such an extent that they raise the Earth's average annual temperature higher than it needs to be. The 1990s were the warmest decade on record. Scientists blame the rise in temperature on the increasing amounts of gases spewed into the atmosphere by human activity. This is the result of burning **fossil fuels** such as gasoline and coal, that produce CO_2.

Global warming shows just how interdependent the countries of the world have become. The solution is obvious: Cut down on the amount of greenhouse gases emitted by factories, coal-burning power plants, and automobiles around the world. Clearly, this is a situation that requires global cooperation.

The Impact of Global Warming on Canada

It is difficult to predict with certainty what the long-term impact of global warming will be on Canada. Some of the conditions Canadians might face are:
▶ more frequent and more severe droughts in the Prairies.
▶ increased rainfall on Canada's coastlines and delta areas (Vancouver, Charlottetown, Halifax, and St. John's).
▶ sea levels rising by 15 cm to 95 cm over the next century. This will create extreme difficulties for low-lying coastal communities like Richmond, B.C. and Charlottetown, P.E.I.
▶ contamination of freshwater supplies by rising saltwater levels.
▶ longer and warmer growing seasons.
▶ a northward movement of boreal forests with grasslands replacing them in the south.
▶ disruption of ocean and freshwater fish stocks.
▶ loss of habitat for animals in wildlife areas.
▶ thawing of permafrost areas in the Arctic.

Not included in the above list is the possible effect on Canada of severe environmental damage in other regions of the world. Remember that Canada's economy depends a great deal on trade with other countries. If global warming causes the economies of some of these countries to collapse, this could have a negative impact on the standard of living in Canada.

How the Greenhouse Effect Works

SOLAR ENERGY

3. About 30% of infrared radiation escapes back into space

Heat trapped by excess carbon dioxide

1. Solar radiation (heat) absorbed by earth

Carbon dioxide released by aircraft

Heat trapped by excess carbon dioxide

4. Heat trapped by excess carbon dioxide

5. Oceans warm, water evaporates and vapor adds to heat trap

Forests cut down

2. Earth's surface radiates heat (infrared radiation) back into atmosphere

Ships burn fossil fuel or oil

Factories release carbon dioxide

Burning of fossil fuels and vehicle exhaust

Figure 28-1 The Greenhouse effect.

Figure 28-2 This power plant produces electricity by burning coal. It also produces large amounts of CO_2, which is the most common of the greenhouse gases responsible for global warming. What can Canadians do to reduce emissions of these gases?

StatScan
Earth's Temperature, 1850-1997

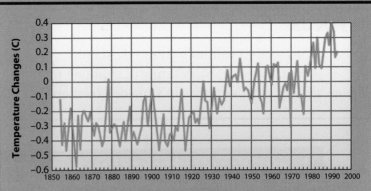

Figure 28-3 Does this graph support those scientists who claim human activity is warming up the planet's climate? What additional information about worldwide energy use and industrial activity would be helpful in backing up this claim?

CaseStudy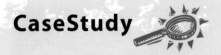

THE KYOTO PROTOCOL ON GLOBAL WARMING

On December 11, 1997 in Kyoto, Japan, 38 industrialized countries including Canada agreed for the first time to reduce their emissions of greenhouse gases. This agreement, called the Kyoto Protocol, was reached after years of meetings sponsored by the United Nations. Representatives from 159 countries attended the 10-day meeting in Kyoto. Environmentalists argued strongly in favour of the agreement, while representatives of the coal, oil, and automobile industries argued against it.

The terms of the Kyoto Protocol include:
- by 2012, industrialized countries must reduce their greenhouse gas emissions by an average of 5.2% below their 1990 levels.
- emission credits for industries that reduce emissions below their target. These emission credits can then be purchased by other industries that exceed their targets. This punishes polluting companies and rewards "clean" ones.
- emission-level reductions apply only to industrialized countries, not developing ones. Developing countries claimed it would be unfair for them to have to reduce emissions at the same time they were trying to improve their economies. Countries with growing greenhouse gas emissions such as India and China are, therefore, outside the scope of the Kyoto Protocol.
- emission credits for countries with forest "sinks." A sink is the term for an area, such a forest, that absorbs CO_2 and, therefore, helps to reduce the amount of greenhouse gases in the atmosphere.

Many of the details of this treaty still need to be worked out. Before it becomes legally binding, the Kyoto Protocol must be ratified by at least 55 countries by March 1999. These 55 countries must largely be drawn from a list of the Earth's worst polluters. This list is composed of the world's most advanced industrial countries—Canada, the U.S., European countries, and Japan. Canada signed the Kyoto Protocol on April 25, 1998 in spite of complaints from oil-and coal-rich Alberta. Alberta had maintained that the Kyoto Protocol would harm its economy to a much greater extent than it would that of any other province in Canada. As of August 25, 1998, 50 countries had ratified the agreement.

RECONNECT

1. What are the possible effects of global warming on Canada? Are they beneficial or harmful? Back up you answer by citing evidence from this section.

2. Is the Kyoto Protocol a good treaty for Canada? Give proof to back up your answer.

FOCUS

This section will help you understand
a. how globalization will continue to influence Canada in the 21st century
b. recent trends in Canada's relations with the global community.

> The explosion of technology has caused a revolution in transportation, communications, and information processing, compressing time and space, erasing national borders, and leading to fundamental economic and social changes. Globalization has created growing interdependence of countries and peoples.
> —Special Joint Committee Reviewing Canadian Foreign Policy Report, Canadian Parliament, January 24, 1995.

Canada and the Global Village

As we saw in Chapter 1, Marshall McLuhan coined the term "global village" more than 35 years ago. He used the term to refer to this planet as a world where various peoples are connected to each other by high-tech communication devices such as telephones, radios, and televisions. Since then computer technology and the Internet have brought the people of McLuhan's global village much closer together than he could have imagined. Not only are people from different countries in touch with each other on a daily basis, but their well-being often depends on these connections.

It is likely that countries which cut themselves off from the global community will not prosper in the 21st century. International companies, called multinationals, have branches in countries around the world. They can expand these branches or shut them down depending on whether or not they receive favourable treatment from local governments. Also, international investors can transfer money from a weak market to a more profitable one in seconds. These are examples of economic interdependence in the world today.

In many ways global interdependence defines Canada as a country. Interdependence has been crucial to Canada's prosperity for much of the 20th century because the country's economy is so dependent on foreign trade. As we saw in earlier chapters, however, there are many other links that

Figure 29-1 An employee labours in a plant in Penang, Malaysia belonging to Baxter Healthcare, a multinational company.

Primary Source
ECONOMIC INTERDEPENDENCE

As one contemplates an ever-changing international economic landscape—the reduction of trade barriers, the integration of markets, the globalization of investment—it becomes increasingly clear that Canada must continue to push its frontiers outward or risk being left behind.

—Roy MacLaren, Canadian Minister for International Trade, 1994.

strengthen Canada's interdependence with the global community. These include political, military, social, cultural, and environmental links.

CANADA'S LINKS TO THE GLOBAL COMMUNITY

United Nations The 185-member UN is the most important forum for discussing and attempting to solve international problems. Its headquarters is in New York City.

NATO During the Cold War, the North Atlantic Treaty Organization was the most important military alliance to oppose the Communist bloc headed by the Soviet Union. Dominated by the U.S., NATO included Canada and most of the countries of Western Europe. With the end of the Cold War, NATO approved the admission in 1997 of three former members of the Communist Bloc: Hungary, Poland, and the Czech Republic.

The Commonwealth A loose, voluntary association of Great Britain and most of its former colonies. The 53-member Commonwealth promotes economic and social development and has pressured member countries to become more democratic.

la Francophonie A loose association of 47 countries where French is spoken and that promotes economic and social development.

NORAD The North American Air Defence was set up originally to guard against attacks by jet bombers and later by intercontinental missiles from the Soviet Union.

APEC The Asia-Pacific Economic Co-operation's main aim is to promote trade and investment among its 21 members.

G-8 The Group of Eight, or G-8, meets regularly to resolve economic issues before they become sources of conflict. Formerly known as the G-7, it first met in 1978. It included seven countries—Canada, the U.S., Germany, France, Great Britain, Japan, and Italy. In 1997 Russia joined making it the G-8.

NAFTA The North American Free Trade Agreement joined the U.S., Canada, and Mexico into the largest free trade zone in the world and will eliminate tariffs on most goods by 2007.

OECD The Organization for Economic Cooperation and Development was founded in 1961 and exists mainly to promote world trade and to help resolve economic problems. It was an outgrowth of the Marshall Plan which the U.S. set up after World War II to distribute economic aid to the countries of war-torn Europe. With headquarters in Paris, the OECD is made up of 29 countries with the world's most advanced economies.

Figure 29-4 Ken Saro-Wiwa, a Nigerian playwright and activist, was executed for criticizing the government. Nigeria was suspended from the Commonwealth following the execution of Saro-Wiwa and eight other dissidents in 1995.

OAS The Organization of American States was founded in 1948 and consists of 35 countries in North and South America that meet periodically to resolve political and economic problems in the region. Its headquarters is in Washington, D.C. In 1962, Communist Cuba was expelled from the OAS. In 1990, Canada finally became a full member of the OAS. Canada had been reluctant to join the OAS over concerns about lack of democracy in many South American countries.

WTO The World Trade Organization includes 132 countries that have agreed to lower trade barriers. The WTO aims to prevent countries from favouring their own companies at the expense of foreign-owned businesses.

Figure 29-3 U.S. President Bill Clinton signing NAFTA in 1992.

Figure 29-2 Most of the international organizations to which Canada belongs have been described in earlier chapters. In most cases they resulted from a treaty signed by Canada and other countries on economic, defence, or cultural issues.

Global Interdependence

Increased global interdependence can have both good and bad effects. For example, the profits from increased trade and investment can provide many Canadians with a better standard of living. On the other hand, cheaper imports from a low-wage country like Mexico can lead to unemployment in Canadian manufacturing industries.

Interdependence can also limit Canada's ability to solve its own problems. For instance, Parliament, by passing a law to assist Canadian companies, might violate an agreement like NAFTA or the WTO. The challenge for Canada is to run its own affairs in a way that benefits Canadians while still dealing with the reality of an interdependent world.

CaseStudy

THE HELMS-BURTON ACT

The Helms-Burton Act is an excellent example of how another country's policies can affect Canadian affairs in an ever increasing climate of global interdependence.

Background

The Helms-Burton Act arises out of a long-standing feud between the U.S. and Cuba which dates back to Fidel Castro's successful revolution in 1959. Castro set up a communist form of government and **nationalized** many American businesses that were located in Cuba. During the Cuban Missile Crisis in 1962 the world teetered on the brink of a nuclear war. Relations between the U.S. and Cuba were strained to the limit. Since then, the U.S. has maintained a trade boycott against Cuba as a way of encouraging the overthrow of its communist government.

The Law

In 1996, the American government passed the Helms-Burton Act. The aim of this law was to force U.S. trading partners like Canada to stop trading with Cuba. The law made it possible for American citizens to sue Canadian companies that invested in Cuba. Many of these citizens were Cubans who had fled their native land after the Cuban Revolution in 1959, and whose property in Cuba was seized by the new government of Fidel Castro. If Cuban refugees felt that a Canadian company was making a profit by using their former property, they could sue the company in an American court. They could also have the company's executives barred from entering the U.S.

Figure 29-5 The neighbourhood of San Miguel Del Pardon in Havana. Partly because of the American trade embargo, Havana is not as technologically advanced as other large cities in North and South America. On September 16, 1996, Canadian Trade Minister Arthur Eggleton remarked, "Helms-Burton is an unwarranted move to extend the arm of U.S. law into trade between other countries."

Outcome

Together with many other countries, the Canadian government has vigorously protested against this American attempt to influence its trading practices. The law is particularly annoying from Canada's point of view since most Canadian multinationals do in fact have offices in the U.S. The U.S. is, after all, Canada's largest trading partner by a wide margin, while Cuba is at best a minor one. Nevertheless, Canada considers that the question of whom it trades with is its own affair. It has maintained that Canadian trade should not be restricted by any other country, not even a superpower like the U.S. As of July 1998, U.S. President Bill Clinton had not enacted the provision of Helms-Burton that would allow Americans to sue Canadian companies.

Primary Source

"AN ENORMOUS DISPARITY OF POWER."

The following statement is from a report submitted to the Canadian parliament on January 24, 1995 by the Special Joint Committee Reviewing Canadian Foreign Policy. The committee was made up of Members of Parliament and Senators. The report describes a modern interdependent world and suggests how Canada should best conduct its foreign policy.

"The freedom of action of every nation is more or less restricted in today's interdependent world, but Canada's is more restricted than most because of its geographic proximity to the United States…There is an enormous disparity of power between the two countries. Consequently the impact of the U.S. on Canada is out of all proportion to the impact of Canada on the U.S."

Canada and the 21st Century

Since the end of the Cold War in the early 1990s, a new world order has been taking shape, one which we have referred to throughout this book as a global community. For Canada, the global community holds both promises and risks.

On the positive side, Canada has benefited from the expansion of the global economy. Thanks to organizations such as the WTO, the European Union, and APEC, governments around the world have agreed to act within a common set of rules that treats all countries fairly.

On the other hand, globalization has increased the influence of multinational companies to such an extent that the power of governments to control their own affairs has been diminished. In some cases, even a country's culture has had to make room for globalization. In the case of Canada, the overwhelming economic and cultural might of the U.S. has sometimes seemed to make a mockery of Canada's attempts to maintain a distinct culture.

Futurists have made conflicting predictions about what might happen in the 21st century. Most see Canada as a country which must earn its livelihood in a world of growing interdependence.

▶ **Prediction 1:** Multinational corporations from the wealthiest five or six countries, led by the U.S., will dominate the global economy. These large corporations will become even more powerful so that most governments in the world will have little room to make independent decisions. In Canada, this will mean that the border with the U.S. will eventually disappear. Canada will be divided up into three or four American states.

▶ **Prediction 2:** Trade and investment will expand greatly around the world. Treaties to promote global trade and investment will include virtually every country. As a result the standard of living will increase in wealthy as well as in developing countries. Canada, aided by a large multicultural population, will especially profit since such a large share of its economy is devoted to trade.

▶ **Prediction 3:** Globalization will increasingly face a backlash in Canada as well as in other parts of the world. Peoples of particular religions and cultures will feel threatened by a barrage of American-inspired culture made possible by satellite links, TV, and the Internet. Violent conflicts will break out as people and governments in some regions of the world attempt to shut off the forces of globalization. Other parts of the world will embrace globalization in all its economic and cultural aspects. This will create two tiers of countries—one which is isolated and another which is interdependent.

▶ **Prediction 4:** Beginning with North America and Europe, and then spreading to Asia, South America and even Africa, cultures will increasingly influence and borrow from each other. With this emerging global culture, international misunderstandings will diminish. The dominant cultural influence will be more American than any other. Canada will have an advantage over most other countries since it already has such close cultural ties to the U.S.

However the globalization forces play out in the 21st century, Canada will most likely have to chart its future in a world of expanding global interdependence.

RECONNECT

1. Which of the above predictions, or parts of them, seem most likely to occur? What other developments are likely to occur? Support your answers by referring to information from previous chapters in this book.

2. In general, do you see globalization as a positive or a negative force for: a) Canada b) your personal future?

GLOSSARY

absolute monarchy a form of government in which the monarch (king, queen, emperor, empress, or the equivalent) holds total power.

annexation the addition of a territory or country to one's own.

apartheid segregation based on race.

arms race the competition among nations to develop and buy weapons.

Asian flu the economic crisis in the Asia Pacific region in 1998.

autonomy self-government.

baby boom the marked increase in the birth rate that began after World War II and continued until the mid-1960s.

balance of trade the difference in value between imports and exports.

boycott a systematic refusal to handle or purchase the goods or services of a particular company.

branch plants businesses owned and controlled by companies with their headquarters in other countries.

bullion gold or silver in bulk before being made into coins.

capitalist a person who believes in an economic system based on private investment and profit making.

Cold War the period between 1945 and 1991 marked by political tension between the Soviet Union and the United States, and the threat of war this created.

commodities raw or partially processed materials such as grain, coffee, wool, or metals.

communist a person who believes in an economic system based on public ownership of all property and on workers being paid according to their needs and abilities.

conscription compulsory military service.

consumerism the promoting of consumer spending or the preoccupation with acquiring consumer goods.

container port a port specializing in handling goods stored in containers.

continentalist a person who believes that Canada and the U.S. should have greater economic, political, and cultural cooperation and favours policies that will be good for the entire continent rather than one country.

Crowsnest Pass Agreement an 1897 agreement that set up a system of transport subsidies for grain shipments. The agreement was meant to help farmers in the western provinces.

demographers people who study the statistics of births, deaths, and disease in human populations.

devaluation the lowering in value of a currency in relation to other currencies so that exports become cheaper and imports become more expensive.

domestic market the market for goods and services within a country.

Doukhobors members of a Russian Christian sect, many of whom migrated to Canada in 1899 after suffering persecution for refusing military service.

environmental degradation the breakdown of the environment cased by pollution and other factors.

exchange rates the value of one currency in terms of another.

European Union the economic association of European nations previously known as the European Community.

fossil fuels oil, coal, and other hydrocarbons deposited in a previous geological age.

franchises stores, restaurants, and so on which are authorized by companies to sell their goods or services.

futurists people who are concerned with or study the future.

global economy the trend towards lower trade barriers and increasing economic links among countries.

global links the trend towards greater links among countries.

globalization the trend towards the expansion of economic activities throughout the world.

greenhouse effect the raising of atmospheric temperatures by the trapping of heat by carbon dioxide, methane, and other gases.

head tax a tax levied on new immigrants to a country.

human rights basic rights, such as freedom of expression or freedom to practise any religion, thought to belong to every person.

interdependent being dependent on each other.

International Monetary Fund (IMF) an international agency that promotes the growth of trade and monetary cooperation, and makes loans to developing countries experiencing debt problems.

Luftwaffe the German air force up to the end of World War II.

martial law the suspension of ordinary law in favour of military rule by the government.

middle power a nation without the military might or wealth to make it a superpower, but with enough resources and the political ability to give it some influence in world affairs.

minority government an elected government in which the governing political party does not hold the majority of the seats in the legislature.

multiculturalism a government policy supporting the development of a variety of cultural values and practices.

multinational corporation a business with offices or plants in several countries.

nationalists people who have a sense of national consciousness and intense loyalty to their country.

nationalized the take over of a private company or industry by the state.

NORAD the North American Air Defence Command. In 1981 NORAD changed its name to the North American Aerospace Defence Command (NAADC).

Pacific Rim the countries and regions bordering the Pacific Ocean sharing political, economic, and environmental interests.

peacekeeping an action by armed forces of the United Nations to maintain a truce between nations or regions which had been at war.

pogroms the organized massacre of the Jews in Russia in the early 20th century.

political repression to suppress any political opposition, often through violent actions.

precedent a previous case that is used as a guide for upcoming cases or as a justification.

primary goods raw materials such as oil, coal, and wood.

quality of life the standard of living and non-material things people have.

recession in economics, the decline in business activity lasting more than six months.

reincarnation the rebirth of a soul in a new body.

resource sector in economics, the part of the economy that deals with natural resources.

retail companies companies that sell goods to the public in small quantities.

rods the metals bars connecting the drawbars of a railway car. Rod is used in the expression "ride the rods" which means hitching a ride on a freight train.

sectors parts of the economy focusing on the production of certain types of services or goods.

sovereignty the political control of a country and a country's right to control its own affairs and borders.

standard of living the quality and quantity of goods and services that people are able to purchase or attain.

Suez Crisis a conflict following the nationalization of the Suez Canal by President Nasser of Egypt in 1956. Britain, which had controlled the Suez Canal, France, and Israel landed troops to regain control, but withdrew them after other countries criticized their actions.

sustainable development economic development that manages the environment and its resources in a way that allows future generations to benefit from them.

tariffs taxes put on goods that enter a country from other countries.

totalitarian a dictatorship that regulates every aspect of private and state behaviour.

trade deficit when a country buys more from a trading partner than it sells.

trade surplus when a country sells more to a trading partner than it buys.

Western alienation the feeling of people in some western provinces of being cut off or separated from other groups, people, or regions.